Raspberry Pi

Amazon Alexa Voice Services, Voice controlled Home computerization, DS18B20 Temperature Sensor, DHT11 Humidity Sensor, MPU6050 Gyro Sensor, Hall Sensor etc,..

CONTENTS

Raspberry Pi

ACKNOWLEDGMENTS

The writer might want to recognize the diligent work of the article group in assembling this book. He might likewise want to recognize the diligent work of the Raspberry Pi Foundation and the Arduino bunch for assembling items and networks that help to make the Internet of Things increasingly open to the overall population. Yahoo for the democratization of innovation!

INTRODUCTION

The Internet of Things (IOT) is a perplexing idea comprised of numerous PCs and numerous correspondence ways. Some IOT gadgets are associated with the Internet and some are most certainly not. Some IOT gadgets structure swarms that convey among themselves. Some are intended for a solitary reason, while some are increasingly universally useful PCs. This book is intended to demonstrate to you the IOT from the back to front. By structure IOT gadgets, the per user will comprehend the essential ideas and will almost certainly develop utilizing the rudiments to make his or her very own IOT applications. These included ventures will tell the per user the best way to assemble their very own IOT ventures and to develop the models appeared. The significance of Computer Security in IOT gadgets is additionally talked about and different systems for protecting the IOT from unapproved clients or programmers. The most significant takeaway from this book is in structure the tasks yourself.

1. INTERFACING DS18B20 TEMPERATURE SENSOR WITH RASPBERRY PI

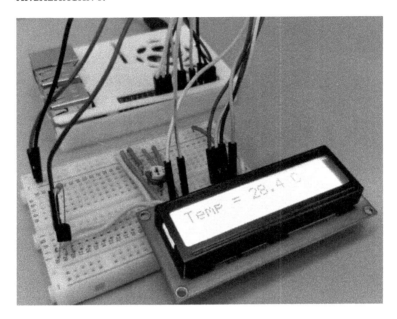

Raspberry Pi is known for its computational power as well as its immense application in the field of Internet of Things, Home Automation and so forth. Anyway for any electronic framework to communicate with this present reality and get data about it, the framework needs to utilize sensors. There are numerous kinds of sensors utilized for this procedure and the necessary sensor is chosen dependent on the parameter to be estimated and its application. In this instructional exercise we figure out how to interface a temperature sensor DS18B20 with the Raspberry Pi.

The DS18B20 is broadly utilized temperature sensor, for the most part at places where brutal working situations are included like compound enterprises, mine plants and so on. This article will tell about the sensor and how it outstands other temperature sensor lastly interface it with Raspberry Pi and view the temperature esteem on the 16x2 LCD.

Materials Required

- DS18B20 Temperature Sensor
- 16*2 LCD display
- Raspberry Pi
- 10k Pull up resistor
- 10k trim pot
- Connecting wires
- Breadboard

Introduction to DS18B20 Temperature Sensor

The DS18B20 is a three terminal temperature sensor accessible in the TO-92 (transistor type) bundle. It is anything but difficult to utilize and requires just a single outside part to begin working. Additionally it requires only one GPIO stick from the MCU/MPU to speak with it. An average DS18B20 temperature sensor with its stick name is demonstrated as follows.

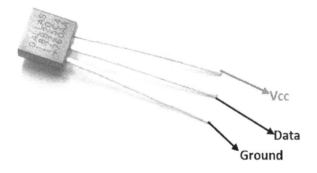

This sensor is additionally accessible as a waterproof

form where the sensor is secured by a round and hollow metal cylinder. In this instructional exercise we will utilize the ordinary transistor type sensor that is appeared previously. The DS18B20 is a 1-wire programmable temperature sensor meaning it requires just the information stick to send the data to the microcontroller or microchip sheets like the Raspberry Pi. Every sensor has a one of a kind location of 64-piece for it so it is likewise conceivable to have numerous sensors associated with the equivalent MCU/MPU since every sensor can be tended to exclusively on similar information transport. The particular of the sensor is appear beneath.

- Working voltage: 3-5V

- Estimating Range: -55°C to +125°C

- Precision: ±0.5°C

- Goals: 9-piece to 12-piece

Since we know enough of the sensor, let us detail interfacing it with Raspberry Pi.
Pre-Requisites

It is expected that your Raspberry Pi is now flashed with a working framework and can interface with the web. If not, pursue the Getting started with Raspberry Pi instructional exercise before continuing. Here we are utilizing Rasbian Jessie introduced Raspberry Pi 3.

It is likewise accepted that you approach your pi

either through terminal windows or through other application through which you can compose and execute python projects and utilize the terminal window.

Circuit Diagram

As we told before in this instructional exercise we will interface the DS18B20 sensor with Pi as well as show the estimation of temperature on a 16*2 LCD screen. So the sensor and the LCD ought to be associated with Raspberry Pi as show beneath.

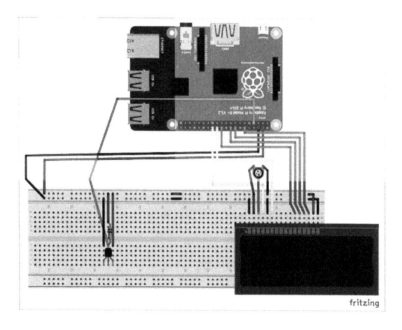

Pursue the circuit graph and make the association in like manner. Both the LCD as well as the DS18B20 sensor works with the assistance of +5V which is given by the 5V stick on the Raspberry pi. The LCD is made to work in 4-piece mode with Raspberry pi, the GPIO pins 18,23,24 as well as 25 is utilized for the information line as well as the GPIO pins 7 as well as 8 is utilized for the control lines. A potentiometer is likewise utilized to manage the difference level of the LCD. The DS18B20's information line is associated with GPIO stick 4. Likewise note that a 10K resistor must be utilized force the information like high as show in the circuit chart.

You can either pursue the circuit chart above and make the associations or go through the stick table to pursue with the GPIO stick numbers.

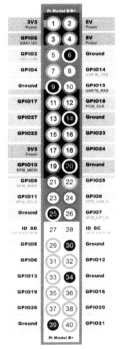

I have constructed the circuit on a breadboard utilizing the single strand wires and male to female wires to make the associations. As should be obvious the sensor requires just one wire to interface and subsequently consumes less space and sticks. My equipment resembles this underneath when every associations are made. Presently it an opportunity to control up the pi and start programming.

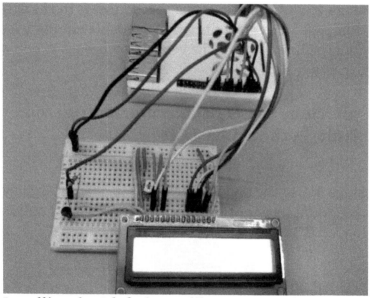

Installing the Adafruit LCD library on Raspberry P

The estimation of the temperature will be shown on a 16*2 LCD show. Adafruit gives us a library to effortlessly work this LCD in 4-piece mode, so let us add it to our Raspberry Pi by opening the terminal window Pi and following the beneath steps.

Stage 1: Install git on your Raspberry Pi by utilizing the beneath line. Git enables you to clone any extend documents on Github and use it on your Raspberry pi. Our library is on Github so we need to introduce git to download that library into pi.

```
apt-get install git
```

Stage 2: The accompanying line connects to the Git-Hub page where the library is available simply execute the line to clone the venture record on Pi home registry

```
git clone git://github.com/adafruit/Adafruit_Python_CharLCD
```

Stage 3: Use the underneath order to change registry line, to get into the task document that we just downloaded. The direction line is given beneath

```
cd Adafruit_Python_CharLCD
```

Stage 4: Inside the catalog there will be a record called setup.py, we need to introduce it, to introduce the library. Utilize the accompanying code to introduce the library

sudo python setup.py install

That is it the library ought to have been introduced effectively. Presently likewise how about we continue with introducing the DHT library which is additionally from Adafruit.
Enabling One-Wire Interface in Pi

Since the DS18B20 sensor conveys through One-Wire strategy, we need to empower the one wire correspondence on Pi by following the beneath steps.

Stage 1:- Open the Commands incite and utilize the underneath order to open the config document

sudo nano /boot/config.txt

Stage 2:- Inside the config record include the line "dtoverlay=w1-gpio" (circled in underneath picture) and spare the document as demonstrated as follows

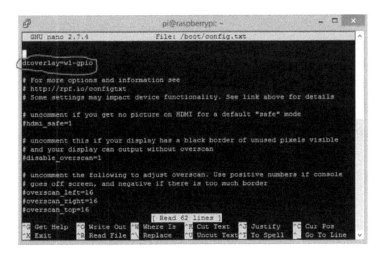

Stage 3:- Use Ctrl+X to leave the document and spare it by squeezing "Y" and afterward Enter key. At long last restart the Pi by utilizing the direction

sudo reboot

Stage 4:- Once rebooted, open the terminal again and enter the accompanying directions.

sudo modprobe w1–gpio

sudo modprobe w1-therm.

cd /sys/bus/w1/devices

ls

Your terminal windows will show something like this

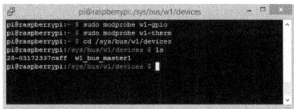

Stage 5:- At the finish of stage 4 when you enter ls, your pi will show a one of a kind number this number will be diverse for every client, in light of the sensor, however will consistently begin with 28-. For my situation the number is 28-03172337caff.

Stage 6:- Now we can check if the sensor is working by entering the accompanying directions

cd 28-XXXXXXXXXXXX [use the name of your directory or use Tab key for auto complete)

cat w1_slave

These two directions will peruse the information from the sensor and show it on the terminal as show beneath. The estimation of temperature is circled with red in the beneath picture. For my situation the estimation of temperature is 37*C.

Programming your Raspberry Pi for DS18B20 Sensor

Presently we have our Pi fit to be modified for LCD and to utilize One-wire convention. So we can compose our last program to peruse the estimation of temperature from the DS18B20 sensor and show it on the LCD screen. The total python program to do the equivalent is given toward the finish of this page. Anyway beneath I have part the code into little significant pieces to clarify them.

As consistently we start the program, by bringing in the header documents required by the program. Here we import time to manage defer work, the LCD header to utilize LCD with Pi. The os header is accustomed to taking care of documents in the OS.

import time #import time for creating delay

import Adafruit_CharLCD as LCD #Import

LCD library

import os #Import for file handling

import glob #Import for global

Next we require to make reference to the LCD pins which are associated with Raspberry Pi Pins. Utilize the GPIO stick graph gave above to realize the stick quantities of the separate GPIO pins. When we have announced, to which pins of PI the LCD is associated with, we can indicate the quantity of lines and sections lastly introduce it by utilizing the beneath lines of code.

lcd_rs   = 7 #RS of LCD is connected to GPIO 7 on PI

lcd_en   = 8 #EN of LCD is connected to GPIO 8 on PI

lcd_d4   = 25 #D4 of LCD is connected to GPIO 25 on PI

lcd_d5   = 24 #D5 of LCD is connected to GPIO 24 on PI

```
lcd_d6      = 23 #D6 of LCD is connected to
GPIO 23 on PI

lcd_d7      = 18 #D7 of LCD is connected to
GPIO 18 on PI

lcd_backlight = 0 #LED is not connected
so we assign to 0

lcd_columns = 16 #for 16*2 LCD

lcd_rows   = 2 #for 16*2 LCD

lcd    =    LCD.Adafruit_CharLCD(lcd_rs,
lcd_en, lcd_d4, lcd_d5, lcd_d6, lcd_d7,

  lcd_columns, lcd_rows, lcd_backlight)
#Send all the pin details to library
```

In the wake of introducing the LCD we print an example instant message on the LCD. The character '\n' is utilized to specify new line. In the wake of showing the introduction we present a deferral of 2 seconds for the client to peruse the introduction message.

```
lcd.message('DS18B20   with   Pi   \n   -
Helloworld) #Give a intro message
```

time.sleep(2) #wait for 2 secs

Presently, in case you could recall the stage 4 of empowering one wire interface with Pi. We need to rehash a similar line of code, so we utilize the os.system capacity to execute similar lines. At that point we indicate the record area from where the estimation of temperature must be perused. The device_folder variable focuses to the envelope that starts with '28-' since we don't have the foggiest idea about the careful name of the organizer we utilize the * image to open whatever that starts with 28. At long last inside that envelope we utilize another variable called device_-file which really indicates the record which has the estimation of temperature inside it.

At that point we use work named get_temp inside which we characterize the system of perusing the temperature from the document that we simply connected in the above advance. As we checked with the terminal before the document will have the estimation of temperature inside it yet it will in the accompanying organization

From this we just need the estimation of 37000, which is the estimation of temperature. Here the genuine estimation of temperature is 37.00*C. So from this arrangement of content we need to trim

all the futile information and get the whole number worth 37000 lastly partition it by 1000 to get the genuine information. The capacity appeared beneath does precisely the equivalent

```
def get_temp(): #Fundtion to read the value of Temperature

    file = open(device_file, 'r') #opent the file

    lines = file.readlines() #read the lines in the file

    file.close() #close the file

    trimmed_data = lines[1].find('t=') #find the "t=" in the line

    if trimmed_data != -1:

        temp_string = lines[1][trimmed_data +2:] #trim the strig only to the temoerature value

        temp_c = float(temp_string) / 1000.0 #divide the value of 1000 to get actual
```

value

return temp_c #return the value to print on LCD

The variable lines is utilized to peruse the lines inside the document. At that point these lines are analyzed scanned for the letter "t =" and the incentive after that letter is spared in the variable temp_string. At last to get the estimation of temperature we utilize the variable temp_c in which we isolate the string an incentive by 1000. At last return the temp_c variable because of the capacity.

Inside the endless while circle, we just need to call the above characterized capacity to get the estimation of temperature and show it in the LCD screen. We additionally clear the LCD for each 1 sec to show the refreshed worth.

while 1: #Infinite Loop

lcd.clear() #Clear the LCD screen

lcd.message ('Temp = %.1f C' % get_ temp()) # Display the value of temperature

time.sleep(1) #Wait for 1 sec then update the values

Output / Working

As consistently the total python code is given toward the end of the page, utilize the code and incorporate it on your Raspberry Pi. Make the association as appeared in the circuit chart and before executing the program ensure you have pursued the above strides to introduce LCD header records and empower one-wire correspondence on pi. When that is done simply execute the program, if everything is filling in true to form you ought to have the option to see the introduction content. If not alter the differentiation potentiometer until you see something. The conclusive outcome will look something like this beneath.

Expectation you comprehended the task and had no

issue building it. This is only an interfacing venture, yet once this is done you can think ahead by chipping away at a Raspberry Pi climate station, temperature E-mail notifier and significantly more.

Code

```
#Program to read the values of Temp from the DS18B20 sensor and display them on the LCD
import time #import time for creating delay
import Adafruit_CharLCD as LCD #Import LCD library
import os #Import for file handling
import glob #Import for global
lcd_rs    = 7 #RS of LCD is connected to GPIO 7 on PI
lcd_en    = 8  #EN of LCD is connected to GPIO 8 on PI
lcd_d4    = 25 #D4 of LCD is connected to GPIO 25 on PI
lcd_d5    = 24 #D5 of LCD is connected to GPIO 24 on PI
lcd_d6    = 23 #D6 of LCD is connected to GPIO 23 on PI
lcd_d7    = 18 #D7 of LCD is connected to GPIO 18 on PI
```

```
lcd_backlight =  0  #LED is not connected so
we assign to 0
lcd_columns = 16 #for 16*2 LCD
lcd_rows   = 2 #for 16*2 LCD
lcd = LCD.Adafruit_CharLCD(lcd_rs, lcd_en,
lcd_d4, lcd_d5, lcd_d6, lcd_d7,
              lcd_columns, lcd_rows, lcd_back-
light)  #Send all the pin details to library
lcd.message('DS18B20    with    Pi   \n   -
Helloworld) #Give a intro message
time.sleep(2) #wait for 2 secs
os.system('modprobe w1-gpio')
os.system('modprobe w1-therm')
base_dir = '/sys/bus/w1/devices/'
device_folder = glob.glob(base_dir + '28*')[0]
device_file = device_folder + '/w1_slave'
def get_temp(): #Fundtion to read the value
of Temperature
  file = open(device_file, 'r') #opent the file
  lines = file.readlines() #read the lines in the
file
  file.close() #close the file
  trimmed_data = lines[1].find('t=') #find the
"t=" in the line
  if trimmed_data != -1:
     temp_string = lines[1][trimmed_data+2:]
#trim the strig only to the temoerature value
```

```
    temp_c = float(temp_string) / 1000.0
#divide the value of 1000 to get actual value
    return temp_c #return the value to prnt
on LCD
while 1: #Infinite Loop
  lcd.clear() #Clear the LCD screen
  lcd.message ('Temp = %.1f C' % get_temp())
# Display the value of temperature
    time.sleep(1) #Wait for 1 sec then update
the values
```

❖ ❖ ❖

2. THE MOST EFFECTIVE METHOD TO SETUP WEBSERVER ON RASPBERRY PI AND HOST A WORDPRESS WEBSITE

A captivating aspect regarding framework on chips (SoC) like Raspberry Pi is their capacity to fill in as web servers to have sites and other online applications. This webserver serves have records when solicitation is produced using the customer end. Today, I exhibit How to Setup a Webserver on Raspberry Pi and Install a Wordpress Website which can be gotten to by any gadget on a similar system as the raspberry pi. Indeed, even you can put Raspberry Pi online by port sending procedure and can get to the site from anyplace on the planet.

Required Component

The accompanying segments are required to assemble this undertaking;

- Raspberry pi 2 otherwise 3
- LAN/Ethernet Cable
- Secure Digital Card (8gb Minimum)

- Power source

- WiFi Adapter (if utilizing the Raspberry pi 2)

Discretionary

- Mouse

- Console

- HDMI Cable

- Screen

To continue, we will utilize the Raspbian stretch OS for this instructional exercise and since its arrangement is same as that of the Jessie, I will expect you know about setting up the Raspberry Pi with the Raspbian stretch OS. I likewise expect you know how to SSH into the Raspberry Pi utilizing a terminal programming like putty.

For new Stretch clients (crisp introduces), you should take note of that SSH is debilitated and you should empower SSH before you can converse with the raspberry pi over SSH. One approach to do this is to initiate it by interfacing a screen and empowering SSH, while the subsequent which is my most loved is by making a record named ssh (with no expansion) and duplicating it to the root envelope on your SD card. This should be possible by embeddings the SD card into your PC.

We will fire the instructional exercise by setting up

the raspberry pi as a web server which can be utilized to have any sort of site after which we will take a gander at setting up a WordPress site on the server.

Likewise check other Raspberry Pi Server for media as well as print server:

- Step by step instructions to Set up Plex Media Server on Raspberry Pi

- Raspberry Pi Print Server

- Step by step instructions to Install Kodi on Raspberry Pi 3

Setup Webserver on Raspberry Pi

There are a few server stacks however for this instructional exercise, we will utilize the LAMP stack which represents Linux, Apache, MySQL as well as PHP.
Step 1: Update the Pi

It is essential to refresh the Pi toward the beginning of any task as this introduces update for every one of the bundles introduced already and guarantees similarity issues don't emerge, when the product bundles required for the new ventures are introduced. To refresh the pi run;

Sudo apt-get update

Sudo apt-get upgrade

Step 2: Install Apache

Since we previously run a Linux machine, the principal thing to be done is to introduce Apache. Apache like most other webserver applications can be utilized to serve HTML record over http or utilized with extra modules and bundles to serve dynamic site pages like most wordpress sites, which are assembled utilizing dialects like PHP.

To introduce apache run;

Sudo apt-get install apache2

With the establishment done, you can test it by visiting the IP address on your program. You should see a page like the one appeared in the picture beneath.

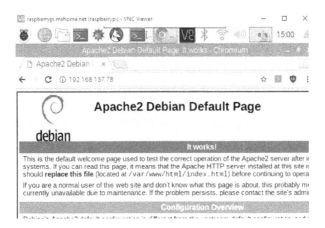

The page appeared above speaks to the html substance of the index.html document situated in the/

var/www/html catalog which was made during the apache establishment.

To show a one of a kind website page or make numerous pages, the substance of the index.html record can be altered to mirror the data to be shown.

To alter the document, we have to change the proprietorship from root to your own username. Accepting your username is the default username "pi" change into the www registry and change the responsibility for record;

cd /var/www/html

sudo chown pi: index.html

With the possession transformed, we would then be able to alter the content utilizing the nano word processor. Run;

Sudo nano index.html

Change the code to mirror whatever changes you want, spare and invigorate the page on the program to see the change.

Step 3: Install PHP

To enable the web server to serve some mind boggling and dynamic website pages, to enable it to process html, CSS JavaScript and PHP we should introduce different parts of the LAMP stack. Since we are as of now running on a Linux machine, the following part of the stack we will introduce is PHP. To introduce, run;

Sudo apt-get install php libapache2-mod-php

With this done, we can test the establishment by making an index.php record and supplement it into the www registry. This ought to be done simply after the index.html record has been expelled from the registry as the .html overshadows .php.

To expel the .html document, while still inside the www index, run;

```
sudo rm index.html
```

Make the index.php record utilizing;

```
sudo nano index.php
```

Supplement some line of PHP code in the record.

```
<?php echo " server up and running";?>
```

Spare and leave the supervisor. Invigorate the page on the program to see the changes.

On the off chance that the crude php content is appeared on the website page rather than the "server ready for action" content, restart the apache server. This is finished utilizing;

```
sudo service apache2 restart
```

You should now have the option to see the substance of the site page appropriately.

Rather than evacuating the index.html page, another page can be made with a name other than list. For eample page.php.

This page can be gotten to on the program by means of http://<youripaddress>/page.php

Step 4: Install MySQL Sever

Next, we have to introduce a database motor to oversee and store information on the server. For the Lamp stack, we will utilize MySQL. We have to introduce MySQL server and the PHP bolster bundles for MySQL. An option in contrast to these will be to utilize PHPmyAdmin.

To introduce the MySQL server run;

Sudo apt-get install mysql-server php-

mysql

With this done, restart Apache utilizing;

sudo service apache2 restart

With this done, you currently have a total web server fully operational and the database should now be administrable. Now, you can make and host a site on this server by putting the html and PHP pages of the site in the www catalog of the webserver and it will be available by anybody on a similar system as the raspberry pi.
Install and Setup WordPress on the Raspberry Pi

With our webserver ready for action one great approach to test what we have done is to introduce the well known Content administration framework WordPress. With this, we will have the option to make a site in a couple of moments minutes.
Step 1: Download and Install WordPress

To clear things up and free some space on the raspberry pi, we evacuate the substance of the www registry. To do this run;

Cd ~

Cd /var/www/html

sudo rm *

Subsequent to erasing every documents, we at that point download WordPress from their official site utilizing;

sudo wget http://wordpress.org/latest.tar.gz

Once the download is finished, extricate the tarball utilizing;

sudo tar xzf latest.tar.gz

Move the substance of the WordPress envelope into the present registry utilizing;

Sudo mv wordpress/* .

Note the space before the "."

At that point evacuate the tarball to free up space on the pi utilizing;

Sudo rm –rf wordpress latest.tar.gz

Before we proceed, we have to change the responsibility for the wordpress records to the apache client. Run;

Sudo chown -R www-data: .

*don't neglect to include the "." after the segment.
Step 2: Setup the DataBase

All sites need a database; this is the place MySQL comes in. To set up a database for WordPress, run;

sudo mysql_secure_installation

You will be incited to enter the default/current secret phrase. Simply press the enter key. Pursue the brief to finish the arrangement by making another secret key (Ensure you utilize a secret phrase you can undoubtedly recall), evacuate mysterious clients, refuse remote root login, expel test database, and reload benefits table. You should see an all done comment when everything is finished.

Next we make a database for WordPress. Run;

sudo mysql -uroot -p

Enter the root secret phrase we made above, you should view a greeting to mariaDB screen brief on the screen. At the point when this shows up, make another DB utilizing the order;

create database wordpress;

Note that the "WordPress" in the order above is my favored name for the DB. Don't hesitate to pick yours.

In the event that this is effective, you should see a screen like the one in the picture beneath.

```
pi@raspberrypi:/var/www/html $ sudo mysql -uroot -p
Enter password:
Welcome to the MariaDB monitor.  Commands end with ; or \g.
Your MariaDB connection id is 10
Server version: 10.1.23-MariaDB-9+deb9u1 Raspbian 9.0

Copyright (c) 2000, 2017, Oracle, MariaDB Corporation Ab and others.

Type 'help;' or '\h' for help. Type '\c' to clear the current input statement.

MariaDB [(none)]> create database wordpress
    -> ;
Query OK, 1 row affected (0.00 sec)

MariaDB [(none)]>
```

Next, award database benefits to the root client utilizing;

GRANT ALL PRIVILEGES ON wordpress.* TO 'root'@'localhost' IDENTIFIED BY 'YOURPASSWORD';

```
Welcome to the MariaDB monitor.  Commands end with ; or \g.
Your MariaDB connection id is 10
Server version: 10.1.23-MariaDB-9+deb9u1 Raspbian 9.0

Copyright (c) 2000, 2017, Oracle, MariaDB Corporation Ab and others.

Type 'help;' or '\h' for help. Type '\c' to clear the current input statement.

MariaDB [(none)]> create database wordpress
    -> ;
Query OK, 1 row affected (0.00 sec)

MariaDB [(none)]> GRANT ALL PRIVILEGES ON wordpress.* TO 'root'@'localhost' IDEN
TIFIED BY '          ' ;
Query OK, 0 rows affected (0.00 sec)

MariaDB [(none)]>
```

For the progressions made to the DB to produce results, we have to flush the database benefits. Run;

FLUSH PRIVILEGES;

With this done, we at that point exit mariaDB utilizing CTRL+D.
Step 3: Configure WordPress

Open an internet browser on the pi and go to http:// localhost you should see a WordPress page requesting that you select your favored language, select your favored language and snap proceed.

On the following page, click on how about we go to continue with establishments.

It will demand for essential site data. Fill them as demonstrated as follows;

Database name: wordpress

Username: root

Password: <insert your password>

Database host: localhost

Table prefix: wp_

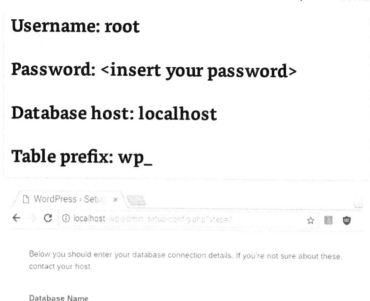

Snap the "submit" button pursued by the "Run the Install" button. This will demand an email, a username and secret key for your site. Supply this data and hit the "introduce wordpress" button. With this done, you should now have the option to login to the backend of the sites and modify its look and use by visiting http://localhost/wp-administrator

To make the URL friendlier for clients seeing from an alternate gadget on a similar system, we will change the permalinks settings. To do this, from the wordpress backend, go to settings, select permalinks, select the "post name" choice and snap on the "spare changes" button.

So the webserver is lined up with these change, we should empower apache's revamp mod. Run;

Sudo a2enmod rewrite

We additionally need to educate the virtual host to enable solicitations to be overwritten. To do this we should alter the default design of the accessible destinations utilizing the nano manager.

Run;

sudo nano /etc/apache2/sites-available/000-default.conf

Include the accompanying lines after the main line

<Directory "/var/www/html">

AllowOverride All

</Directory>

Guarantee it's inside the <VirtualHost *: 80> casing as demonstrated as follows.

<VirtualHost*: 80>

<Directory "/var/www/html">

AllowOverride All

</Directory>

...

Spare the document and leave utilizing CTRL+X pursued by Y and enter.

Restart Apache to impact the progressions made to the setup records. Run;

Sudo service apache2 restart

That is it, we have site running on our Raspberry web-server. WordPress can be effectively altered to your taste. You can without quite a bit of a stretch change topics, include pages, posts, change the menu and so forth.

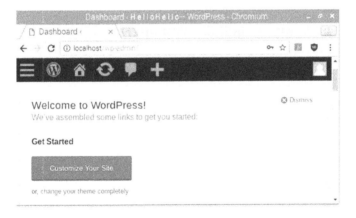

For the most part, there are parcel of things that can be accomplished with a private webserver. One of those key uses is for document sharing between gadgets associated on a similar system as the server.

By associating the raspberry pi to a switch and utilizing port sending procedures, the webserver can be conveyed to serve website pages on the web. This implies the records put away on the webserver can be gotten to from anywhere on the planet.

It ought to be noticed that the raspberry pi as an equipment is constrained and may not perform ideally whenever used to have sites with high traffic.

3. VOICE CONTROLLED HOME COMPUTERIZATION UTILIZING AMAZON ALEXA ON RASPBERRY PI

Have you at any point considered a speaker which can be constrained by your voice!!! Consider the possibility that we can control our home apparatuses thusly and make these machines more intelligent. Voice colleagues getting increasingly famous as we are going towards a time of AI as well as Internet of Things based frameworks. You have found out about Google Assistant, Apple Siri and Amazon Alexa. These all are Voice based AI frameworks, what makes these not quite the same as one another is their environments, and this is the place Amazon Alexa champion the most. Google, Apple and Amazon, every one of these organizations previously propelled their keen speakers however Amazon was first to present them.

Amazon reverberation, Echo Dot Spot, and so forth are the shrewd speakers which are accessible in showcase.

Amazon gives the API to utilizing its much well known voice administration, Alexa. It is open source and accessible on Github. Further you can introduce or incorporate Alexa on custom gadgets like Raspberry Pi and get the full Amazon Echo usefulness in that gadget.

Utilizing Alexa voice administration, we can play music, get data about climate, book tickets and some more. You should simply inquire. In past instructional exercise we have controlled Raspberry Pi GPIO utilizing Amazon Alexa. In this instructional exercise, how about we perceive how to construct a voice controlled home robotization framework utilizing Amazon Alexa and Raspberry Pi. We will perceive how we can utilize Raspberry Pi to run the Alexa Voice Service as well as control a Light Bulb.

Perquisite Material:

Hardware Requirements:

- External Speaker with 3.5mm AUX cable
- Raspberry Pi 3 [Recommended] or Raspberry Pi 2 Model B [Supported] as well as Secure Digital Card (8GB or more)
- Relay module
- Any Webcam or Universal Serial Bus 2.0 Microphone
- LED/ AC Bulb

Note: Webcam has inbuilt amplifier thus, we will utilize this instead of USB 2.0 receiver.

Programming Apps and Web Requirements:

- Register a record with Alexa Voice Services
- Register a record with PubNub
- Register a record with IFTTT

We additionally accept that your Raspberry pi is as of now set up with a Raspbian OS and is associated with the web. With these set up we should continue with the instructional exercise. In the event that you are new to Raspberry Pi, at that point experience Getting started with Raspberry pi first.

The entire instructional exercise is mostly isolated into 5 sections, which are as per the following:

- On the off chance that you don't have screen, at that point we need to arrangement the Raspberry Pi with SSH and VNC, likewise check the USB Microphone network.

- Set up Your Amazon Developer and introducing Alexa on Raspberry Pi

- Setting up PubNub and IFTTT for Alexa Home Automation

- Equipment association

- Python code for Alexa Pi Home Automation

So lets begin!!

Part 1: Setting up the Raspberry Pi with SSH and VNC

To start with, we will interface Raspberry Pi with SSH and VNC. For this pursue instructional exercises on authentic Raspberry Pi's site, joins are given underneath.

For SSH: SSh interface

For VNC : VNC interface

In case you have Monitor, at that point you can leave this progression and go legitimately to stage 2 which is Setting Up The Alexa Voice Service(Avs). Before that we need to check mic network.

Checking Webcam Mic with Raspberry Pi:

1. Open Raspberry Pi terminal as well as type arecord -l order. This will show the equipment gadgets which are associated with Raspberry Pi as demonstrated as follows:

Card 1 is your webcam's mic that we are gonna to utilize. On the off chance that it isn't shown, your webcam might be faulty.

2. Presently, check if mic is working by running the record sound direction as :

arecord /home/pi/Desktop/test.wav -D sysdefault:CARD=1

3. To play the recorded sound sort this direction :

```
omxplayer -p  -o  local /home/pi/Desk-
top/test.wav
```

In the event that you have associated Raspberry Pi with screen utilizing HDMI link, at that point as a matter of course sound yield is through your screen's speaker (if there is inbuilt speaker in it). Along these lines, to transform it to 3.5mm you need to type the accompanying order:

```
sudo raspi-config and go to Advance op-
tion.
```

Select Audio from the rundown - > select Force 3.5mm - > select Ok and Restart you Raspberry Pi.

Presently, you ought to hear the sound from 3.5mm jack.

NOTE: If you require to increment or abatement the information voice uproar for mouthpiece the sort alsamixer in the terminal. Select sound card from the terminal by squeezing F6.

Press F4 to change the Mic dB pick up and set it as you need.

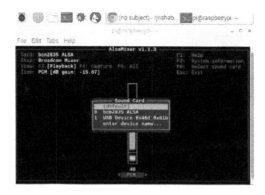

In the event that you have USB 2.0 amplifier, at that point steps pursued are same to check the mouth-piece. Here we have utilized Webcam for USB micro-cphone.

Part 2: Set up Your Amazon Developer Account and Configure Alexa Voice Services on Raspberry Pi:

We have just clarified this in detail in our past instructional exercise where we have assembled an Amazon Echo savvy speaker. Here are we are concentrating on controlling Home Appliances with Alexa so we are not clarifying the entire procedure once more, so read the past article and prepare your Speaker with Alexa voice administrations introduced on your Raspberry pi.

To test Alexa, simply wake her up by saying her name!

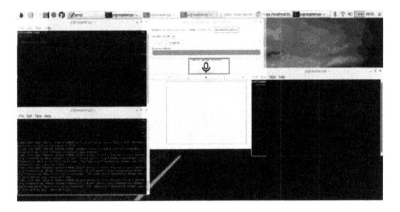

You can get some information about temperature of your city to check it is working or not.

Part 3: Setting up PubNub and IFTTT for Alexa Pi Home Automation:

For building home computerization framework utilizing this Alexa Pi, we need the assistance of PubNub python SDK and IFTTT. We will offer directions to IFTTT through Alexa, as well as PubNub offers sign to RPi to On/Off the light. So we will initially introduce the PubNub on Raspberry Pi.

Section 3-1: Installing PubNub Python SDK:

PubNub gives an informing API to distribute/buy in any message on their Global system. Here we are utilizing IFTTT as well as Alexa to distribute the message on PubNub, for turning On/Off the Relay. This message is gotten by Raspberry Pi and Pi will kill On or the Light as needs be. Pursue beneath steps to arrangement PubNub on Raspberry Pi:

1.Open terminal on your RPi as well as run the accompanying direction to introduce SDK:

sudo pip install pubnub==3.9.0

Introduce 3.9.0 form just, other rendition won't work with the python content which we will going to run in the last.

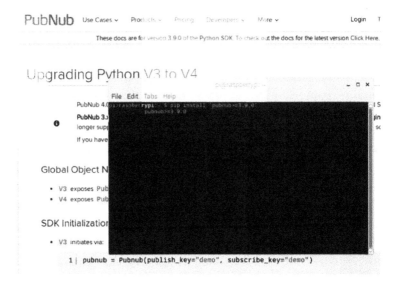

2. Presently, go to PubNub and sign in with your accreditations.

ANBAZHAGAN K

3. Acquire the Publish as well as Subscribe Keys we will utilize later on.

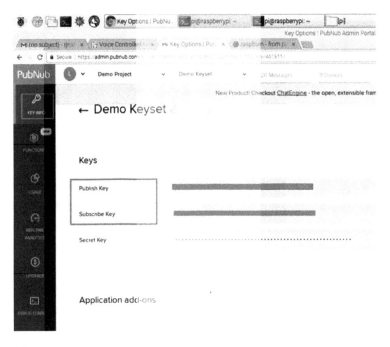

58

Part 3-2: Setting up IFTTT for Amazon Alexa Service:

IFTTT is a free electronic assistance that enables clients to make chains of basic contingent articulations, called "plans", which are activated dependent on changes to other web administrations, for example, Gmail, Facebook, Instagram, and Pinterest. IFTTT is a shortened form of "In the event that This, Then That".

For this undertaking, IFTTT is utilized to trigger the light switch on/off directions dependent on the discourse order got by Alexa administration running on RPi.

Pursue these means to make an Applet:

Stage 1:- Login to IFTTT with your certifications or Sign Up on the off chance that you don't have a record on it.

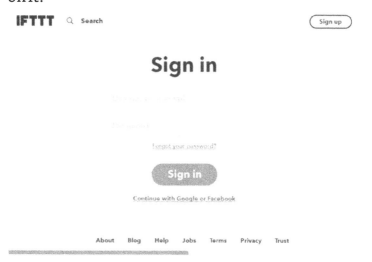

Stage 2:- On My Applets, Click on New Applet

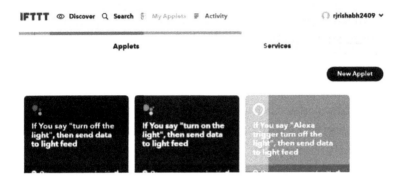

Stage 3:- Click on +this

Stage 4:- Search Amazon Alexa and snap on it, sign in with your amazon designer account subtleties.

Stage 5:- Choose the trigger, Say a particular expres-

sion

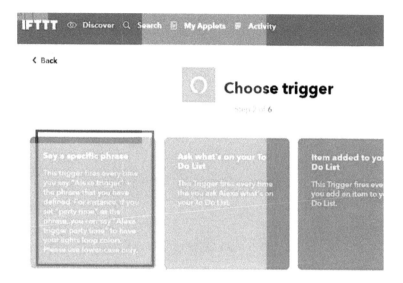

Stage 6:- Provide "turn on the light" as the expression, click on Create Trigger.

Complete trigger fields

Step 2 of 6

Say a specific phrase

This trigger fires every time you say "Alexa trigger" + the phrase that you have defined. For instance, if you set "party time" as the phrase, you can say "Alexa trigger party time" to have your lights loop colors. Please use lower case only.

What phrase?

turn on the light

Use lower case characters only

Create trigger

Stage 7:- Click on +that

if ◯ then ➕ that

Stage 8:- Search for Webhooks, click on it and Select Make a Web Request

Stage 9:- Webhooks gives the REST WEB Request, Use the Publish and Subscribe keys got from the PubNub and alter the accompanying URL.

http://pubsub.pubnub.com//distribute/pub_key/ sub_key/0/alexaTrigger/0/{"requester":"Alexa","trigger":"light","status":1}

Stage 10:- Paste the adjusted URL to the URL content box.

Complete action fields

Step 5 of 6

Stage 11:- Set the Method as GET, Content as application/json and click on spare.

Stage 12:- Follow similar strides to make the trigger for "turn off the light" and change the URL to the accompanying.

http://pubsub.pubnub.com//distribute/pub_key/ sub_key/0/alexaTrigger/0/{"requester":"Alexa","trigger":"light","status":0

Review and finish

Step 6 of 6

If You say "Alexa trigger turn on the light", then make a web request

69/140

by rjrishabh2409

works with

Stage 13:- We are currently prepared with all the web parts for the demo.

Part 4: Hardware connections and Circuit Diagram:

For this undertaking, we need a Relay Module and AC bulb or some other AC segment or you can utilize straightforward LED for testing reason. The following is the circuit chart and Hardware associations with control the AC Appliance with Amazon Alexa.

We will utilizing GPIO 18 in our python content along these lines, associate hand-off to GPIO 18. You can change this in python content.

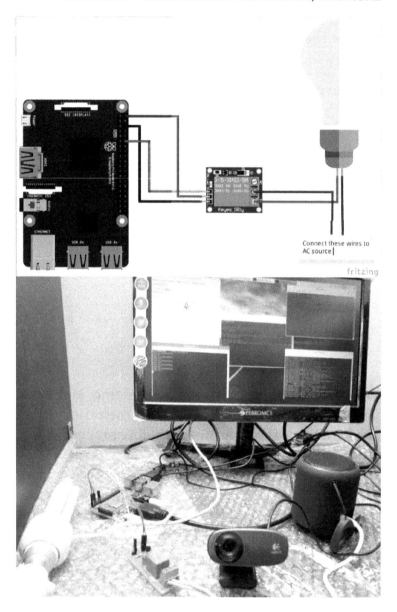

Part 5: Python Code for Controlling the Light:

Locate the total Python Script toward the finish of this instructional exercise.

You have to alter Pub and Sub key with your pubnub enters in the python code.

Initialize the Pubnub Keys

pub_key = "****************************"

sub_key = "**************************"

Presently run the Script

python alexaRpi.py

Presently we are good to go for the demo, Make sure you are running all the three administrations from the Part 1 (the three terminals) before proceeding.

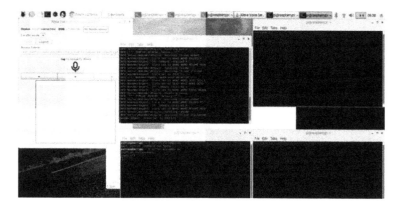

To give any order you have to wake up Alexa administration by calling "Alexa" each time you need to send a direction. You will hear a signal sound. When you hear the blare, say "Alexa Trigger Turn on the Light." You can see the light turns ON inside a minute. And afterward on the off chance that you state "Alexa Trigger Turn off the Light", the light should kill.

That is it…. You can include more AC machines in the python content by including them with other GPIO pins of RPi and can control numerous apparatuses with your savvy home robotization framework.

Check the total code underneath. Additionally check our everything the Home Automation Projects here.

Code

#Import all the libraries
import RPi.GPIO as GPIO

```
import time
from pubnub import Pubnub
# Initialize the Pubnub Keys
pub_key = "*****************************"
sub_key = "**************************"
LIGHT = 18        #define pin of RPi on which
you want to take output
def init():        #initalize the pubnub keys and
start subscribing
 global pubnub   #Pubnub Initialization
 GPIO.setmode(GPIO.BCM)
 GPIO.setwarnings(False)
 GPIO.setup(LIGHT,GPIO.OUT)
 GPIO.output(LIGHT, False)
  pubnub  =  Pubnub(publish_key=pub_key,
subscribe_key=sub_key)
  pubnub.subscribe(channels='alexaTrigger',
callback=callback,    error=callback,    recon-
nect=reconnect, disconnect=disconnect)
def           control_alexa(controlCommand):
#this function control Aalexa, commands re-
ceived and action performed
 if(controlCommand.has_key("trigger")):
  if(controlCommand["trigger"] == "light" and
controlCommand["status"] == 1):
   GPIO.output(LIGHT, True)
   print "light is on"
```

```python
 else:
  GPIO.output(LIGHT, False)
  print "light is off"
 else:
  pass
def callback(message, channel):        #this
function waits for the message from the
aleatrigger channel
 if(message.has_key("requester")):
  control_alexa(message)
 else:
  pass
def error(message):            #if there is error
in the channel,print the  error
 print("ERROR : " + str(message))
def reconnect(message):        #responds if
server connects with pubnub
 print("RECONNECTED")
def disconnect(message):        #responds if
server disconnects with pubnub
 print("DISCONNECTED")
if __name__ == '__main__':
 init()            #Initialize the Script
```

4. HOW TO BUILD A RASPBERRY PI FM TRANSMITTER

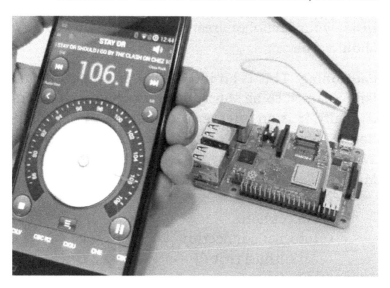

Be it an exhausting evening, a repetitive activity or a desolate lengthy drive FM radio broadcasts have constantly kept us engaged. While on the opposing it ought to likewise be concurred that occasionally these FM stations get exceptionally exhausting with the RJ gabbing unessential stuff or some pestering commercials and that may have kept you think about why you can't have your own FM Broadcast station to air your voice and music over a short separation.

Astounding enough with the assistance of Raspberry Pi it ought to barely take not exactly 30 minutes to set up your very own FM broadcasting station and jump on air inside a neighborhood. With the assistance of an appropriate reception apparatus you ought to have the option to cover a region of 50m Radius which ought to be sufficient to communicate inside your school or area. Fascinating right!! So how about we begin.

Cautioning: This is an instructive examination and isn't planned to be abused for raising a ruckus. Additionally it is an offense to meddle with neighborhood FM frequencies, so utilize this with obligation. We take no property for any setbacks.

Material Required
- Raspberry Pi
- Microphone
- Internet connection
- An enthusiastic RJ

Pre-necessities

It is expected that your Raspberry Pi is as of now flashed with a working framework and can associate with the web. If not, pursue the Getting started with Raspberry Pi instructional exercise before continuing. Here we are utilizing Rasbian Jessie introduced Rasbperrry Pi 3.

It is additionally expected that you approach your Pi either through terminal window or through some victual server like VNC. In this instructional exercise we will utilize the putty terminal window to execute the program on Raspberry Pi.

How Raspberry Pi works as an FM broadcast Station (Transmitter)

One basic inquiry that may emerge in everybody's brain is that by what method can Raspberry Pi a board which is planned to be a chip advancement Board can go about as a FM Transmitter with no extra equipment?

Each microchip will have a synchronous computerized framework related with it which is utilized to diminish the electromagnetic impedance. This EMI concealment is finished by a sign called Spread-range clock sign or SSCS for short. The recurrence of this sign can differ from 1MHz to 250MHz which fortunately for us falls inside the FM band. So by composing a code to perform recurrence balance utilizing the spread-range clock signal we can change the Pi to fill in as a FM transmitter. The balanced sign will be given out through the GPIO stick 4 of the Raspberry Pi. We can basically append a typical wire of 20 cm most extreme to this stick to go about as a radio wire. Setting up the Raspberry Pi for programming

In the event that you definitely realize how to arrive at your pi however Terminal window, at that point avoid this progression, else read through. When you have flashed another OS into your Pi boot it by associating the HDMI out to a screen and furthermore interface a Keyboard and Mouse to your Pi.

At the point when you enter the work area of PI, scan for organize alternative and associate your Pi to your switch. At that point get into pi menu and select pi arrangement and afterward empower permit SSH correspondence. Presently on get onto your windows/MAC PC and interface your PC to a similar switch so your Pi and Laptop takes a shot at the nearby system. Presently introduce Putty and open it. Enter the IP address of the Pi and snap on enter. On the off chance that you don't have a clue about the IP address of PI get into your switch administrator page and check what IP is allotted to your PI, it ought to be something like 192.168.43.XXX. On the off chance that everything is done well a terminal window will spring up requesting username and secret phrase. Of course the username will be pi and the secret word will be raspberry. Enter it and press enter you will get the accompanying screen.

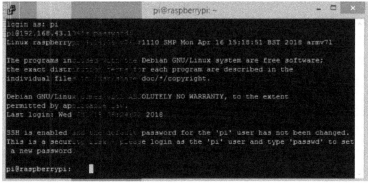

Converting Pi into FM transmitter

The program to change over the PI in to a FM transmitter is now given by Markondej at GitHub page. You can legitimately clone this page into your pi, incorporate the program and dispatch it in case you realize how to do it. For other people, simply pursue the means beneath and you will communicate your own sounds in a matter of moments.

Stage 1: Create a New Folder (index) inside which we will put all our necessary program documents. Here I am utilizing the terminal window to make a registry called PI_FM by utilizing the direction mkdir PI_FM and moving into it by utilizing the order compact disc PI_FM.

mkdir PI_FM

cd PI_FM

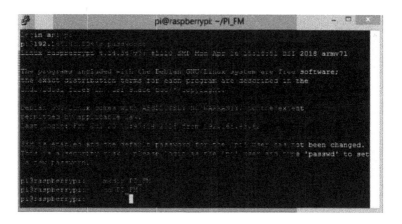

Stage 2: Now we need to clone (download) the program from GitHub into the catalog that we just made. Since we have just moved in the registry, we can simply run the underneath direction to carry out the responsibility and you ought to get the screen appeared here

sudo git clone https://github.com/markondej/fm_transmitter

Stage 3: The program that we just downloaded is a C code, so we need the reasonable compilers and instruments to arrange this program and dispatch it. The compilers for this program is called as gcc and g++ and the apparatus to aggregate them is called make. Utilize the accompanying code to download compilers. Your screen will resemble this beneath once the download is finished

sudo apt-get install gcc g++ make

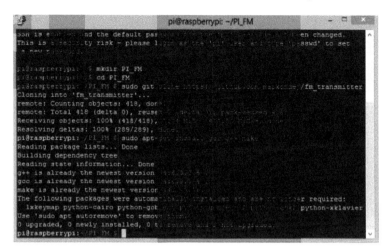

Stage 4: Now we have everything prepared to gather the program. To do that get into the downloaded index by utilizing disc fm_transmitter then accumulate the code utilizing the line sudo make. You program ought to get accumulated and you will get the accompanying screen.

cd fm_transmitter

sudo make

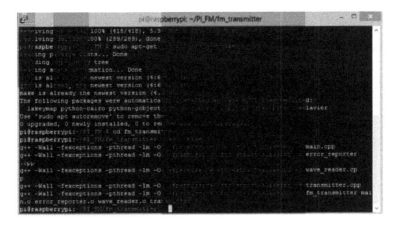

Stage 5: The last advance is dispatch the program. While propelling the program we need to make reference to the recurrence at which we need to communicate and the name of the sound document whcih we need to play. Obviously, there will be a sound record downloaded alongside the program called star_wars.wav. So we will play this stars wars signature music at a 100MHz recurrence to check of the Program works. The syntex for the dispatch line is

sudo ./fm_transmitter [-f frequency] [-r] filename

Since we need 100MHz recurrence and play the star_wars.wav record the line will be

sudo ./fm_transmitter -f 100   -r star_

wars.wav

Testing your Raspberry Pi FM Transmitter

When you have propelled the program and you get the playing message as appeared above we can append a recieving wire to the GPIO stick 4 of the Pi, I have utilized a typical attach wire and it worked fine for me. The image of my set-up is demonstrated as follows.

Presently, all that is left to do it to do is get a FM radio and tune it to 100MHz recurrence and you ought to have the option to hear the communicated star wars music. When you have tried the working, you can supplant the star wars subject with any of your ideal music or voice recording and play it utilizing a similar direction utilized in stage 5.

Broadcasting live voice using Pi

While it is enjoyable to play pre-recorded music cuts, it would be all the more engaging on the off chance that we can communicate live voice utilizing you Pi. This can likewise be accomplished utilizing a simi-lar program. Essentially associate an amplifier to the USB port of Pi and change the dispatch order line. You can allude the github page for more data on this.

5. RASPBERRY PI GPIO CONTROL UTILIZING AMAZON ALEXA VOICE SERVICES

Have you at any point pondered a speaker which can be constrained by your voice!!! Imagine a scenario where we can control our home apparatuses along these lines and make these machines more intelligent. Voice collaborators getting increasingly well known as we are going towards a time of AI and IoT based frameworks. You have caught wind of Google Assistant, Apple Siri and Amazon Alexa. These all are Voice based AI frameworks, what makes these unique in relation to one another is their environments, and this is the place Amazon Alexa champion the most. Google, Apple and Amazon, every one of these organizations previously propelled their savvy speakers yet Amazon was first to present brilliant speakers. Amazon reverberation, Echo Dot Spot, and so forth are the keen speakers which are accessible in advertise.

Amazon gives the API to utilizing its much well known voice administration, Alexa. It is open source and accessible on Github. Further you can introduce or coordinate Alexa on custom gadgets like Raspberry Pi and get the full Amazon Echo usefulness in that gadget.

Utilizing Alexa voice administration, we can play music, get data about climate, book tickets and some more. You should simply 'inquire'. In this instructional exercise, we will perceive how we can control Raspberry Pi GPIO utilizing Alexa Voice administrations to shine a LED.

Perquisite Material:

Equipment Requirements:

- Raspberry Pi 3 [Recommended] or Raspberry Pi 2 Model B [Supported] as well as Secure Digital Card (8GB or more)

- Any Webcam or USB 2.0 Microphone

- Outside Speaker with 3.5mm AUX link

- Driven

- Hand-off module

Note: Webcam has inbuilt amplifier thus, we will utilize this instead of USB 2.0 mouthpiece.

Webcam is used as USB Microphone

Programming Apps and Web Requirements:

- Register a record with Alexa Voice Services
- Register a record with PubNub
- Register a record with IFTTT

We likewise accept that your Raspberry pi is as of now set up with a Raspbian OS and is associated with the web. With these set up we should continue with the instructional exercise. On the off chance that you are new to Raspberry Pi, at that point experience Getting started with Raspberry pi first.

The entire instructional exercise is essentially isolated into 5 sections, which are as per the following:

- In case you don't have screen, at that point we need to arrangement the Raspberry Pi with SSH and VNC, likewise check the USB Microphone availability.

- Set up Your Amazon Developer and introducing Alexa on Raspberry Pi

- Setting up PubNub and IFTTT for Alexa Home Automation

- Equipment association

- Python code for Alexa Pi GPIO Control

In the event that you just needs to control a LED with your voice, the likewise check our Bluetooth based Voice controlled LED venture.

Part 1: Setting up the Raspberry Pi with SSH and VNC

Initially, we will associate Raspberry Pi with SSH and VNC. For this pursue instructional exercises on authentic Raspberry Pi's site, joins are given beneath.

For SSH: SSh connect

For VNC : VNC connect

On the off chance that you have Monitor, at that point you can leave this progression and go straightforwardly to stage 2 which is Setting Up The Alexa Voice Service(Avs). Before that we need to check mic network.

Checking Webcam Mic with Raspberry Pi:

1. Open Raspberry Pi terminal as well as type arecord -l order. This will show the equipment gadgets which are associated with Raspberry Pi as demonstrated as follows:

Card 1 is your webcam's mic that we are gonna to utilize. On the off chance that it isn't shown, your webcam might be faulty.

2. Presently, check if mic is working by running the record sound direction as:

arecord /home/pi/Desktop/test.wav -D sysdefault:CARD=1

3. To play the recorded sound sort this direction:

> ## omxplayer -p -o local /home/pi/Desk-top/test.wav

On the off chance that you have associated Raspberry Pi with screen utilizing HDMI link, at that point as a matter of course sound yield is through your screen's speaker (if there is inbuilt speaker in it). Thus, to transform it to 3.5mm you need to type the accompanying direction:

> ## sudo raspi-config and go to Advance option.

Select Audio from the rundown - > select Force 3.5mm - > select Ok and Restart you Raspberry Pi.

Presently, you ought to hear the sound from 3.5mm jack.

NOTE: If you need to increment or decline the information voice commotion for receiver the sort alsamixer in the terminal. Select sound card from the terminal by squeezing F6.

Press F4 to change the Mic dB pick up and set it as you need.

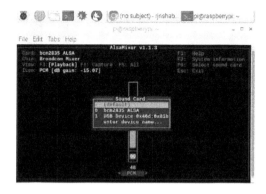

In the event that you have USB 2.0 amplifier, at that point steps pursued are same to check the mouthpiece. Here we have utilized Webcam for USB microcphone.

Part 2: Set up Your Amazon Developer Account and Configure Alexa Voice Services on Raspberry Pi:

We have just clarified this in detail in our past instructional exercise where we have assembled an Amazon Echo savvy speaker. Here are we are concentrating on controlling Raspberry Pi GPIO with Alexa so we are not clarifying the entire procedure once more, so read the past article and prepare your Speaker with Alexa voice administrations introduced on your Raspberry pi.

To test Alexa, simply wake her up by saying her name!

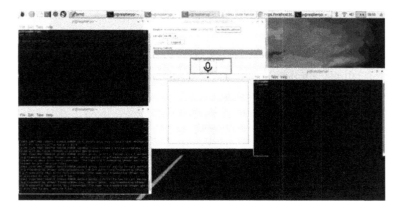

You can get some information about temperature of your city to check it is working or not.

Part 3: Setting up PubNub and IFTTT for Alexa Pi Home Automation:

For controlling Raspberry Pi GPIO utilizing this Alexa Pi, we require the assistance of PubNub python SDK as well as IFTTT. We will offer directions to IFTTT through Alexa, and PubNub offers sign to RPi to turn on/off the LED. So we will initially introduce the Pub-Nub on Raspberry Pi.

Section 3-1: Installing PubNub Python SDK:

PubNub gives an informing API to distribute/buy in any message on their Global system. Here we are utilizing IFTTT and Alexa to distribute the message on PubNub, for making Raspberry Pi GPIO low/high.

This message is gotten by Raspberry Pi and Pi will kill On or the LED as needs be. Pursue beneath steps to arrangement PubNub on Raspberry Pi:

Stage 1: Open terminal on your RPi and run the accompanying order to introduce SDK:

```
sudo pip install pubnub==3.9.0
```

Introduce 3.9.0 form just, other adaptation won't work with the python content which we will going to run in the last.

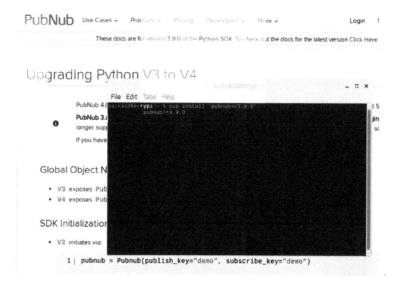

Stage 2: Now, go to PubNub and sign in with your accreditations.

Stage 3:. Acquire the Publish as well as Subscribe Keys we will utilize later on.

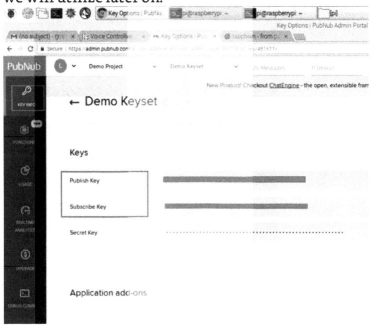

Part 3-2: Setting up IFTTT for Amazon Alexa Service:

IFTTT is a free electronic assistance that enables clients to make chains of straightforward contingent explanations, called "plans", which are activated dependent on changes to other web administrations, for example, Gmail, Facebook, Instagram, and Pinterest. IFTTT is a shortening of "On the off chance that This, Then That".

For this venture, IFTTT is utilized to make the Raspberry Pi GPIO LOW/HIGH dependent on the discourse order got by Alexa administration running on RPi.

Pursue these means to make an Applet:

Stage 1:- Login to IFTTT with your qualifications or Sign Up in the event that you don't have a record on it.

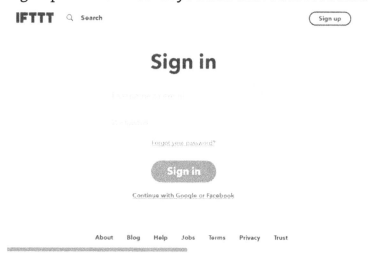

Stage 2:- On My Applets, Click on New Applet

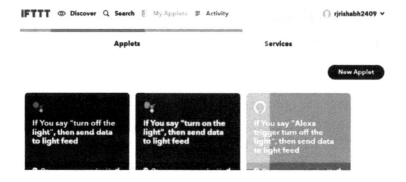

Stage 3:- Click on +this

Stage 4:- Search Amazon Alexa and snap on it, sign in with your amazon engineer account subtleties.

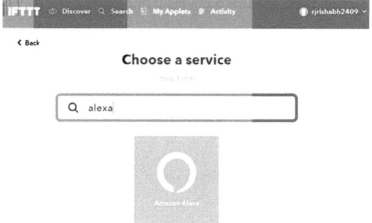

Stage 5:- Choose the trigger, Say a particular expression

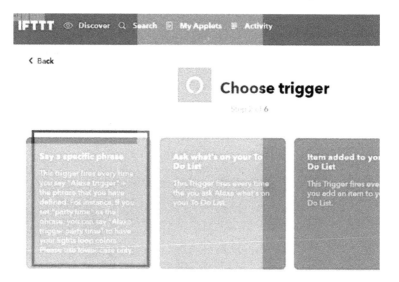

Stage 6:- Provide "turn on the light" as the expression, click on Create Trigger.

Complete trigger fields

Step 2 of 6

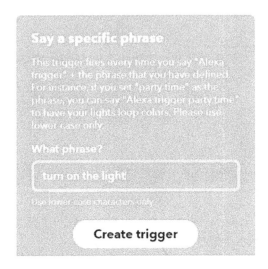

Say a specific phrase

The trigger fires every time you say "Alexa trigger" + the phrase that you have defined. For instance, if you set "party time" as the phrase, you can say "Alexa trigger party time" to have your lights loop colors. Please use lower-case only.

What phrase?

turn on the light

Use lower-case characters only

Create trigger

Stage 7:- Click on +that

About   Blog   Help   Jobs   Terms   Privacy   **Trust**

Add your service and become a partner

IFTTT Platform

Stage 8:- Search for Webhooks, click on it and Select Make a Web Request

Stage 9:- Webhooks gives the REST WEB Request, Use the Publish and Subscribe keys got from the PubNub and alter the accompanying URL.

http://pubsub.pubnub.com//distribute/pub_key/ sub_key/0/alexaTrigger/0/{"requester":"Alexa","trigger":"light","status":1}

Stage 10:- Paste the changed URL to the URL content box.

Complete action fields

Step 5 of 6

Stage 11:- Set the Method as GET, Content as application/json and click on spare.

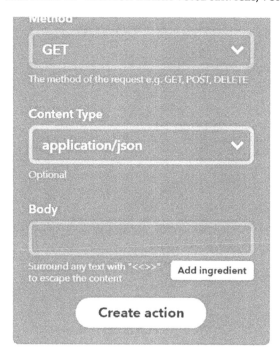

Stage 12:- Follow similar strides to make the trigger for "turn off the light" and change the URL to the accompanying.

http://pubsub.pubnub.com//distribute/pub_key/ sub_key/0/alexaTrigger/0/{"requester":"Alexa","trigger":"light","status":0

Review and finish

Step 6 of 6

Stage 13:- We are currently prepared with all the web parts for the demo.
Part 4: Hardware connections and Circuit Diagram:

For this undertaking, we need a straightforward LED for testing reason. The following is the circuit outline and Hardware associations with controlling Raspberry Pi GPIO with Amazon Alexa.

We will utilizing GPIO 18 in our python content thus, interface hand-off your LED 18. You can change this in python content.

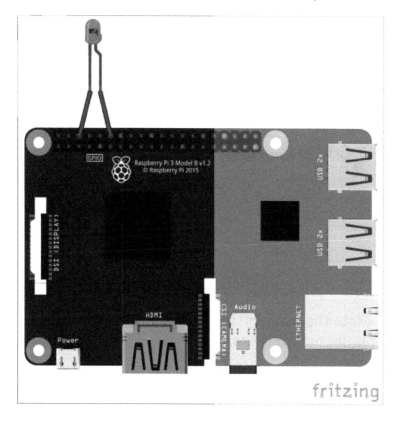

Part 5: Python Code for Controlling the LED:

Locate the total Python Script toward the finish of this instructional exercise.

You have to alter Pub and Sub key with your pubnub enters in the python code.

Initialize the Pubnub Keys

pub_key = "*****************************"

sub_key = "**************************"

Presently run the Script

python alexaRpi.py

Presently we are good to go for the demo, Ensure you are running all the three administrations from the Part 1 (the three terminals) before proceeding.

To give any direction you have to wake up Alexa administration by calling "Alexa" each time you need to send an order. You will hear a signal sound. When you hear the signal, say "Alexa Trigger Turn on the Light." You can see the light turns ON inside a minute. And afterward on the off chance that you state "Alexa Trigger Turn off the Light", the light should kill.

That is it... . You can additionally add a transfer to control AC machine, even you can control numerous apparatuses by utilizing more transfers and more GPIO pins of Raspberry pi.

Check the total code is given underneath. Addition-

ally check our everything the Home Automation Projects here.

Code

```
#Import all the libraries
import RPi.GPIO as GPIO
import time
from pubnub import Pubnub
# Initialize the Pubnub Keys
pub_key = "**************************"
sub_key = "*************************"
LIGHT = 18        #define pin of RPi on which
you want to take output
def init():        #initalize the pubnub keys and
start subscribing
 global pubnub    #Pubnub Initialization
 GPIO.setmode(GPIO.BCM)
 GPIO.setwarnings(False)
 GPIO.setup(LIGHT,GPIO.OUT)
 GPIO.output(LIGHT, False)
  pubnub = Pubnub(publish_key=pub_key,
subscribe_key=sub_key)
  pubnub.subscribe(channels='alexaTrigger',
callback=callback, error=callback, recon-
nect=reconnect, disconnect=disconnect)
def        control_alexa(controlCommand):
```

```
#this function control Aalexa, commands received and action performed
if(controlCommand.has_key("trigger")):
    if(controlCommand["trigger"] == "light" and controlCommand["status"] == 1):
     GPIO.output(LIGHT, True)
     print "light is on"
    else:
     GPIO.output(LIGHT, False)
     print "light is off"
   else:
    pass
def callback(message, channel):        #this function waits for the message from the aleatrigger channel
   if(message.has_key("requester")):
    control_alexa(message)
   else:
    pass
def error(message):          #if there is error in the channel,print the error
   print("ERROR : " + str(message))
def reconnect(message):         #responds if server connects with pubnub
   print("RECONNECTED")
def disconnect(message):         #responds if server disconnects with pubnub
```

```python
print("DISCONNECTED")
if __name__ == '__main__':
 init()          #Initialize the Script
```

❖ ❖ ❖

6. CONSTRUCT YOUR VERY OWN AMAZON ECHO UTILIZING A RASPBERRY PI

It's been very nearly a long time since amazon discharged the Amazon ECHO voice controlled speaker and the notoriety of the speaker has kept on taking off for reasons which are presumably not a long way from the astonishing exhibition of the Alexa voice administration and the way that the stage was opened up to engineers which has prompted the improvement of Alexa good gadgets by top hardware producers and the introduction of a few Alexa/amazon reverberation based tech new companies. Therefore, in the present Article, I will tell you the best way to construct your own DIY rendition of the Amazon reverberation and setting up the Alexa voice administration on the raspberry pi.

Be you a designer or a producer, this will be a chance to acquaint yourself with the fundamental rules that characterizes how the amazon reverberation functions which will come in helpful should you choose

to construct a gadget dependent on the Amazon Echo or the Alexa voice administration.
Required components:

Coming up next are required to fabricate this Raspberry pi amazon reverberation venture:

- Raspberry pi 3 otherwise 2

- Amplifier

- WiFi Dongle (If raspberry pi 2 is to be utilized)

- 5V, 2A Universal Serial Bus Power supply

- Line-in Speaker (with 3.5mm jack)

- Ethernet link

Discretionary Requirements

- Screen

- HDMI CABLE

- Mouse and Keyboard

Since it was taking unreasonably long for the USB mouthpiece I intended to use for this task to show up, I chose to utilize a headset associated with the USB amplifier and headphone connector for my PlayStation 3. In case you can't get the USB mouthpiece like me, you can utilize some other gadget with an amplifier yield like most USB webcams.

This instructional exercise will be founded on the Raspbian stretch OS, so to continue as regular I will expect you know about setting up the Raspberry Pi with the Raspbian stretch OS, and you know how to SSH into the raspberry pi utilizing a terminal programming like putty. In the event that you have issues with any of this, there are huge amounts of Raspberry Pi Tutorials on this site can help.

Because of the idea of this instructional exercise, it is essential to have the option to utilize a visual showcase like a screen or view the raspberry pi work area utilizing VNC. The explanation behind this is to make replicating of IDs from the Amazon site to the terminal.

Step 1: Ready the Pi

This instructional exercise will be in steps to make it simpler to pursue and recreate.

Before beginning any Raspberry Pi venture in the wake of introducing the OS, I like running a report on the pi to guarantee everything on it is modern.

To do that, run:

sudo apt-get update

sudo apt-get upgrade

Step 2: Configure the Sound system of the Pi

At this stage, I will counsel to interface a screen or associate with the work area of your Raspberry Pi utilizing VNC to make things simpler.

With the Pi work area fully operational, interface the receiver over USB and the speaker to the 3.5mm sound jack on the Raspberry Pi. We have to reconfigure the raspberry pi to send sound yield over the 3.5mm jack. To do this, right snap on the sound (speaker) button on the raspberry pi's work area taskbar and select simple as appeared in the picture beneath.

This will enable the Raspberry Pi to send sound out by means of the 3.5mm jack as opposed to sending over HDMI.

Next, we have to design the Raspberry Pi to utilize the associated USB receiver as default. To do this we have to alter the design of the propelled linux sound engineering of the raspberry pi.

We do this utilizing:

sudo nano /usr/share/alsa/alsa.conf

The editorial manager opens up, look to the line for the PCM card and change it from 0 to 1 as appeared in the picture beneath

Spare the setup and leave utilizing ctrl+x
Step 3:- Set up Your Amazon Developer Account

The following stage is for us to make an amazon designer account in order to acquire the engineer IDs, authentications and security profile required for us to have the option to interface with the amazon Alexa voice administration.

Start by heading off to the amazon's designer's site and making a record, you can pursue this connection, click on sign in it will lead you the page to make your engineer account.

When that is done, pursue this connect to the landing page for the designers. I had a few issues exploring the amazon site, so I'd exhort you pursue this connections.

At the landing page, click on the Alexa voice administration featured beneath.

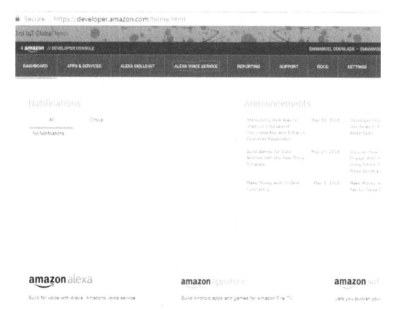

On the following page, click on the Create Product button, featured in the picture beneath;

Fill the item structure as clarified beneath.

Product Name:- RPi Echo (this name is a personal preference, you can use whatever name you desire)

Product ID: RPiEcho (you can use what-ever name you want as product ID).

Product Type: Select Alexa enabled device

Companion App: select No

Product category: select Other

Product description: whatever comes to mind

How users will interact: select hands free

Image Upload: upload any descriptive image or skip.

Commercial distribution: select No

For children: select No

Product name *

RPi Echo

Product ID *

RPiEcho

Please select your product type. *

Alexa-Enabled Application

A standalone app. This includes apps on the web, Android, Kindle, iOS, FireTV, AppleTV, etc.

● **Alexa-Enabled Device**

Physical product with the potential to have buttons, knobs, a touch screen, etc. Examples are speakers, televisions, set top boxes, appliances, etc.

Will your device use a companion app? *

● **Yes**

No

Product category *

Other (please specify)

Raspberry Pi Project

Brief product description *

Installing Alexa on the raspberry pi

In case of filling the structure, click on the following catch toward the finish of the page. On the following page, you will be approached to choose a security profile, pick the Create New Profile alternative.

Enter a profile name and an appropriate portrayal and hit the following catch.

When the following catch is clicked, the security profile ID, the customer ID and the customer mystery will be created. Protect these subtleties as we will utilize them later.

Before you click on the completion button, we have to include ways for the Allowed birthplace and Allowed return URL.

To the Allowed starting point, include the accompanying connections:

- http://localhost:3000

- https://localhost:3000

To the permitted return url, include the accompanying connections:

- https://localhost:3000/authresponse

- http://localhost:3000/authresponse

With these connections included, click on the completion button, as demonstrated as follows.

With the Amazon designer account made and all the necessary IDs procured, we at that point continue to introduce the Alexa voice administration on the raspberry pi.

Step 4: Install and Configure the Alexa Voice Service

on the Raspberry Pi

To introduce the Alexa voice administration on the raspberry pi, we clone the alexa git center point repo by running:

git clone https://github.com/alexa/alexa-avs-sample-app.git

With the repo cloned, change into its index by running;

cd alexa-avs-sample-app.git

We have to design the Alexa voice administration before running the establishment. To do this, we alter the automated_install.sh record;

sudo nano automated_install.h

Fill in the necessary item ID, customer ID and Client mystery data as appeared in the picture beneath.

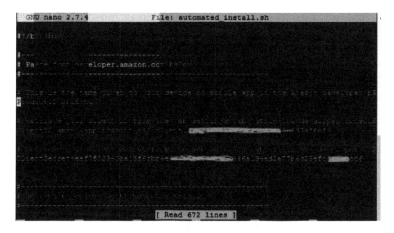

Use ctrl+x to spare and leave the editorial manager.

Next, we have to make the automated_install content an executable record in order to introduce it on the raspberry pi. To do this run;

Sudo chmod+x automated_install.h

After which we run the establishment utilizing;

./automated_install.h

This will introduce the Alexa voice administration on the pi. During the establishment, a few inquiries will emerge that you should give answers to.

You will likewise be approached to choose the sound yield among the inquiries, guarantee to choose the

ANBAZHAGAN K

3.5mm sound jack.

This take few minutes yet after it, you will have the Alexa voice administration introduced.
Step 5: Get the companion app and start AVS Client:

Prior to beginning the AVS, we have to get the buddy application fully operational. The buddy application fills in as a type of door to permit association between our customer and the AVS server.

To begin the buddy, we have to change into the avs test application index and run the going with partner administration. This should be possible by running:

cd   ~/alexa-avs-sample-app/samples/com-panionService && npm start

```
p  :raspberry:  :  /alexa-avs-samp
p  :raspberry:  ~ $ cd ~/alexa-avs-sample-app/samples/companionService && npm sta
 t
> alexa-voice-service-sample-con
mple-app/samples/companionService
> node ./bin/www

This node service needs to be ru
 them for the AVS app.

Listening on port 3000
Successfully retrieved registrat
Successfully retrieved access to
498f3b4a
```

With the partner administration running, we have to begin the AVS customer, to do this, we open another terminal without shutting the one on which the buddy administration is running.

On the new terminal, summon the AVS customer by running;

cd ~/alexa-avs-sample-app/samples/javaclient && mvn exec:exec

Quickly you run the order, you should see a spring up (demonstrated as follows) that requests that you validate the gadget duplicate the connection and glue in an internet browser or snap the yes button.

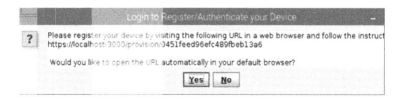

123

When yes has been clicked, don't tap the alright catch on the following discourse box that will spring up until you have finished the confirmation on the website page.

The internet browser may raise a banner and announce the connection unreliable, however advance. The connection will lead you to the amazon engineer account login page, when you sign in, you will be diverted to a page(shown beneath) that affirms verification.

device tokens ready

You would now be able to tap the alright on the exchange box I referenced before. With this, Alexa is prepared for use, every one of the catches on the customer discourse box will currently be empowered so you can snap to give directions to Alexa and get a reaction.

Step 6: Activate Alexa wake word:

The exact opposite thing we will cover in this instructional exercise is initiating the tangible Alexa wake word operator, you will concur with me that clicking a catch constantly to speak with Alexa is kind of not cool. While distinctive wake specialist exists, for this undertaking, we will utilize the Sensory Alexa wake word operator. The wake specialist will run out of sight, sitting tight for us to make reference to the wake word "alexa", when it hears the wake word, it educates our Alexa customer to begin tuning in for directions.

To introduce the wake word specialist, with the customer terminal still up, run the order beneath on another terminal:

> *cd ~/alexa-avs-sample-app/samples/wake-*
> *WordAgent/src && ./wakeWordAgent -e*
> *sensory*

in the event that everything is as it ought to be, you ought to get a reaction like the one underneath.

With this you ought to have the option to get Alexa to hear you out by saying the alexa wake word.

That is it for this instructional exercise folks, there are a few different things you can stack up on your DIY raspberry pi amazon reverberation, I will attempt to cover the majority of them in next barely any instructional exercises if time licenses. Take the undertaking for a turn and tell me how it goes.

Additionally, check our other comparative Raspberry Pi ventures:

- Plex Media Server on Raspberry Pi

- Raspberry Pi Print Server

- The most effective method to Install Kodi on Raspberry Pi 3

- Raspberry Pi Surveillance Camera with Motion Capture

7. INTERFACING DHT11 TEMPERATURE AND HUMIDITY SENSOR WITH RASPBERRY PI

Temperature and Humidity are the most well-known parameters that are being observed in any condition. There are huge amounts of sensors to browse for estimating temperature and stickiness, however the most utilized one is the DHT11 because of its not too bad estimating extent and exactness. It likewise works with one stick correspondence and thus is anything but difficult to interface with Microcontrollers or Microprocessors. In this instructional exercise we will figure out how to interface the well known DHT11 sensor with Raspberry Pi and show the estimation of temperature and stickiness on a 16x2 LCD screen. We previously utilized it to assemble Internet of Things Raspberry Pi Weather Station.

Overview of DHT11 Sensor:

The DHT11 sensor can gauge relative moistness and temperature with the accompanying particulars

Temperature Range: 0-50°C

Temperature Accuracy: ±2 °C

Humidity Range: 20-90% RH

Humidity Accuracy: ±5 %

DHT11 Temperature and Humidity Sensor

The DHT11 sensor is accessible either in module structure or in sensor structure. In this instructional exercise we are utilizing the module type of the sensor, the main contrast between both is that in module structure the sensor has a separating capacitor and a dismantle up resistor appended to the yield stick of the sensor. So on the off chance that you are utilizing the sensor alone ensure you include these two parts. Additionally learn DHT11 interfacing with Arduino.

How DHT11 Sensor functions:

The DHT11 sensor accompanies a blue or white shading packaging. Inside this packaging we have two significant parts which help us to detect the relative mugginess and temperature. The principal part is a couple of anodes; the electrical opposition between these two terminals is chosen by a dampness holding substrate. So the deliberate opposition is contrarily corresponding to the overall dampness of nature. Higher the relative mugginess lower will be the estimation of obstruction and the other way around. Likewise note that Relative moistness is not same as real dampness. Relative dampness gauges the water content in air comparative with the temperature noticeable all around.

The other segment is a surface mounted NTC Thermistor. The term NTC represents Negative temperature coefficient, for increment in temperature

the estimation of obstruction will diminish
Pre-Requisites:

It is expected that your Raspberry Pi is as of now flashed with a working framework and can interface with the web. If not, pursue the Getting started with Raspberry Pi instructional exercise before continuing.

It is likewise accepted that you approach your pi either through terminal windows or through other application through which you can compose and execute python projects and utilize the terminal window.
Installing the Adafruit LCD library on Raspberry Pi:

The estimation of the temperature and mugginess will be shown on a 16*2 LCD show. Adafruit gives us a library to effortlessly work this LCD in 4-piece mode, so let us add it to our Raspberry Pi by opening the terminal window Pi and following the underneath steps.

Stage 1: Install git on your Raspberry Pi by utilizing the underneath line. Git enables you to clone any extend documents on Github and use it on your Raspberry pi. Our library is on Github so we need to introduce git to download that library into pi.

```
apt-get install git
```

Stage 2: The accompanying line connects to the Git-

Hub page where the library is available simply execute the line to clone the undertaking record on Pi home registry

git clone git://github.com/adafruit/Adafruit_Python_CharLCD

Stage 3: Use the beneath order to change index line, to get into the venture document that we just downloaded. The direction line is given beneath

cd Adafruit_Python_CharLCD

Stage 4: Inside the catalog there will be a document called setup.py, we need to introduce it, to introduce the library. Utilize the accompanying code to introduce the library

sudo python setup.py install

That is it the library ought to have been introduced effectively. Presently likewise how about we continue with introducing the DHT library which is additionally from Adafruit.

Installing the Adafruit DHT11 library on Raspberry Pi:

DHT11 Sensor works with the rule of one-wire framework. The estimation of temperature and dampness is detected by the sensor and afterward transmitted through the yield stick as sequential information. We would then be able to peruse these information by utilizing I/O stick on a MCU/MPU. To see how these qualities are perused you would need to peruse the datasheet of the DHT11 sensor, however for the time being to keep things straightforward we will utilize a library to converse with the DHT11 sensor.

The DHT11 library gave by Adafruit can be utilized for DHT11, DHT22 and other one wire temperature sensors too. The system to introduce the DHT11 library is additionally like the one pursued for introducing LCD library. The main line that would change is the connection of the GitHub page on which the DHT library is spared.

Enter the four direction lines individually on the terminal to introduce the DHT library

git clone https://github.com/adafruit/Adafruit_Python_DHT.git

cd Adafruit_Python_DHT

sudo apt-get install build-essential python-dev

sudo python setup.py install

When it is done you will have both the libraries effectively introduced on our Raspberry Pi. Presently we can continue with the equipment association.
Circuit Diagram:

The total circuit outline Interfacing DH11 with Raspberry pi is given underneath, it was fabricated utilizing Fritzing. Pursue the associations and make the circuit

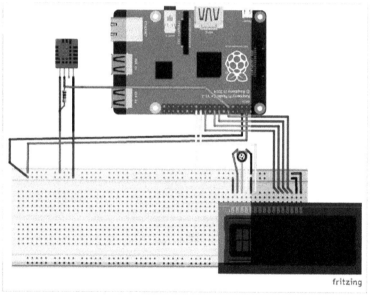

Both the LCD and DHT11 sensor works with +5V supply so we utilize the 5V sticks on the Raspberry Pi to control both. A draw up resistor of significant worth 1k is utilized on the yield stick of the DHT11 sensor, in case you are utilizing a module you can keep away from this resistor.

A trimmer pot of 10k is added to the Vee stick of the LCD to control the differentiation level of the LCD. Other than that every one of the associations are entirely straight forward. Be that as it may, make a note of which GPIO pins you are utilizing to associate the pins since we will require in our program. The beneath graph ought to enable you to make sense of the GPIO stick numbers.

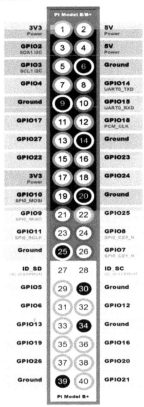

Utilize the graph and make your associations as per the circuit chart. I utilized a breadboard as well as jumper wires to make my associations. Since I utilized DHT11 module I wired it straightforwardly to Raspberry Pi. My equipment resembled this beneath

Python Programming for DHT11 sensor:

We need to compose a program to peruse the estimation of temperature and moistness from the DHT11 sensor and afterward show the equivalent on the LCD. Since we have downloaded libraries for both LCD and DHT11 sensor the code ought to be essentially straight forward. The python complete program can be found toward the finish of this page, yet you can peruse further to see how the program functions.

We need to import the LCD library and DHT11 library

ANBAZHAGAN K

into our program to utilize the capacities identified
with it. Since we have just downloaded and introduced them on our Pi we can essentially utilize the
accompanying lines to import them. We additionally
import the time library to utilize the postpone work.

**import time #import time for creating
delay**

**import Adafruit_CharLCD as LCD #Import
LCD library**

**import Adafruit_DHT #Import DHT Li-
brary for sensor**

Next, we need to indicate to which sticks the sensor is associated with and what sort of temperature
sensor is utilized. The variable sensor_name is appointed to Adafruit_DHT.DHT11 since we are utilizing the DHT11 sensor here. The yield stick of the sensor is associated with GPIO 17 of the Raspberry Pi and
subsequently we relegate 17 to sensor_pin variable as
demonstrated as follows.

**sensor_name = Adafruit_DHT.DHT11 #we
are using the DHT11 sensor**

sensor_pin = 17 #The sensor is connected

to GPIO17 on Pi

Thus, we additionally need to characterize to which GPIO pins the LCD is associated with. Here we are utilizing the LCD in 4-piece mode subsequently we will have four information pins and two control pins to interface with the GPIO pins of the pi. Additionally, you can associate the backdrop illumination stick to a GPIO stick in case we wish to control the backdrop illumination moreover. In any case, until further notice I am not utilizing that so I have appointed 0 to it.

lcd_rs = 7 #RS of LCD is connected to GPIO 7 on PI

lcd_en = 8 #EN of LCD is connected to GPIO 8 on PI

lcd_d4 = 25 #D4 of LCD is connected to GPIO 25 on PI

lcd_d5 = 24 #D5 of LCD is connected to GPIO 24 on PI

lcd_d6 = 23 #D6 of LCD is connected to GPIO 23 on PI

lcd_d7 = 18 #D7 of LCD is connected to GPIO 18 on PI

lcd_backlight = 0 #LED is not connected so we assign to 0

You can likewise associate LCD in 8-piece mode with Raspberry pi yet then free sticks will be diminished.

The LCD library from Adafruit that we downloaded can be utilized for a wide range of trademark LCD shows. Here in our task we are utilizing a 16*2 LCD show so we are referencing the quantity of Rows and Columns to a variable as demonstrated as follows.

lcd_columns = 16 #for 16*2 LCD

lcd_rows = 2 #for 16*2 LCD

Presently, that we have pronounced the LCD pins and the quantity of Rows and Columns for the LCD we can introduce the LCD show by utilizing the accompanying line which sends all the necessary data to the library.

lcd = LCD.Adafruit_CharLCD(lcd_rs, lcd_en, lcd_d4, lcd_d5, lcd_d6, lcd_d7,

lcd_columns, lcd_rows, lcd_backlight) #Send all the pin details to library

To begin the program, we show a little introduction message utilizing the lcd.message() capacity and afterward give a postponement of 2 second to make the message clear. For imprinting on the second line the direction \n can be utilized as demonstrated as follows

lcd.message('DHT11 with Pi \n - Helloworld) #Give a intro message

time.sleep(2) #wait for 2 secs

At last, inside our while circle we should peruse the estimation of temperature and moistness from the sensor and show it on the LCD screen for like clockwork. The total program inside the while circle is demonstrated as follows

while 1: #Infinite Loop

mugginess, temperature = Adafruit_DHT.read_retry(sensor_name, sensor_pin) #read from sensor and spare individual qualities in temperature and dampness varibale

```
lcd.clear() #Clear the LCD screen

    lcd.message ('Temp = %.1f C' % tem-
perature) # Display the value of tempera-
ture

    lcd.message ('\nHum = %.1f %%' % hu-
midity) #Display the value of Humidity

    time.sleep(2) #Wait for 2 sec then up-
date the values
```

We can without much of a stretch get the estimation of temperature and dampness from the sensor utilizing this single line underneath. As should be obvious it return two qualities which is put away in the variable stickiness and temperature. The sensor_name and sensor_pin subtleties are passed as parameters; these qualities were refreshed in the start of the program

moistness, temperature = Adafruit_DHT.read_retry(sensor_name, sensor_pin)

To show a variable name on the LCD screen we can utilize the identifiers like &d, %c and so forth. Here since we are showing a drifting point number with just a single digit after the decimal point we utilize the identifier %.1f for showing the incentive in the variable temperature and moistness

lcd.message ('Temp = %.1f C' % temperature)

lcd.message ('\nHum = %.1f %%' % humidity)

Measuring Humidity and Temperature using Raspberry Pi:

Make the associations according to the circuit outline and introduce the necessary libraries. At that point dispatch the python program given toward the finish of this page. Your LCD should show an introduction message and afterward show the present temperature and moistness esteem as appeared in the picture beneath.

On the off chance that you don't discover anything being shown the LCD, check if the python shell window is showing any erros, in the event that no mistake is shown, at that point check your associations again and change the potentiometer to shift the differentiation level of the LCD and check in the event that you get anything on the screen.

Expectation you comprehended the venture and delighted in building it.

You can likewise check our different activities utilizing DHT 11 with other microcontroller.

Code

#Program to read the values of Temp and Hum from the DHT11 sensor and display them on the LCD

import time #import time for creating delay
import Adafruit_CharLCD as LCD #Import LCD library
import Adafruit_DHT #Import DHT Library for sensor

sensor_name = Adafruit_DHT.DHT11 #we are using the DHT11 sensor
sensor_pin = 17 #The sensor is connected to GPIO17 on Pi

lcd_rs   = 7 #RS of LCD is connected to GPIO 7 on PI
lcd_en   = 8 #EN of LCD is connected to GPIO 8 on PI
lcd_d4   = 25 #D4 of LCD is connected to GPIO 25 on PI
lcd_d5   = 24 #D5 of LCD is connected to GPIO 24 on PI
lcd_d6   = 23 #D6 of LCD is connected to GPIO 23 on PI
lcd_d7   = 18 #D7 of LCD is connected to GPIO 18 on PI

```
lcd_backlight =  0  #LED is not connected so
we assign to 0
lcd_columns = 16 #for 16*2 LCD
lcd_rows   = 2 #for 16*2 LCD
lcd = LCD.Adafruit_CharLCD(lcd_rs, lcd_en,
lcd_d4, lcd_d5, lcd_d6, lcd_d7,
            lcd_columns, lcd_rows, lcd_back-
light)  #Send all the pin details to library
lcd.message('DHT11 with Pi \n -Helloworld)
#Give a intro message
time.sleep(2) #wait for 2 secs
while 1: #Infinite Loop


    humidity, temperature = Adafruit_D-
HT.read_retry(sensor_name,     sensor_pin)
#read from sensor and save respective values
in temperature and humidity varibale
   lcd.clear() #Clear the LCD screen
   lcd.message ('Temp = %.1f C' % tempera-
ture) # Display the value of temperature
   lcd.message ('\nHum = %.1f %%' % humid-
ity) #Display the value of Humidity
    time.sleep(2) #Wait for 2 sec then update
the values
```

8. INTERFACING HALL SENSOR WITH RASPBERRY PI

Lobby sensors will be sensors which creates an electrical sign at its yield when it interacts with an attractive field. The simple estimation of the electric sign at the yield of the sensor is a component of the quality of the attractive field. Corridor sensors are wherever nowadays, they are being utilized for various reasons and in all sort of gadgets from cell phones to switches, for the estimation of speed, position and separation in vehicles and in other car industry based items. This flexibility of corridor sensor makes them an unquestionable requirement have for creators and electrical designers that is the reason today, I will tell us the best way to utilize a Hall Sensor in a Raspberry Pi Based Project.

You can whenever check our other Hall Sensor based tasks, including interfacing of lobby sensor with Arduino.

Required components

The accompanying segments/parts are required to construct this venture;

- Raspberry pi 2 or 3
- SD card (8gb Minimum)
- Hall Effect Sensor
- Jumper wires
- Breadboards
- LAN Cable
- Power source

Some optional parts that may be used include:

- Monitor
- Keyboard and Mouse
- HDMI cable
- Wi-Fi Dongle

Hall Sensor A3144

This instructional exercise will be founded on the Raspbian stretch OS, so to continue as regular I will accept you know about setting up the Raspberry Pi with the Raspbian stretch OS, and you know how to SSH into the raspberry pi utilizing a terminal programming like putty. On the off chance that you have issues with any of this, there are huge amounts of Raspberry Pi Tutorials on this site can help.

For the individuals who will introduce the Raspbian stretch OS just because, one issue I have found, the vast majority have, is getting into the Raspberry Pi by means of ssh. It ought to be noticed that ssh is initially debilitated on the OS and you will require either a screen to empower it, or under the raspberry pi's setup choices or you make a clear document named ssh utilizing your windows or Linux PC and duplicate the clear record to the root index of the SD card. You should embed the SD truck into the SDd card space of your PC to duplicate to it.

Utilizing the subsequent technique is progressively reasonable for those running the pi in headless mode. With every one of the parts prepared we would then be able to continue to building.
Circuit Diagram:

For utilizing Hall impact sensor with Raspberry Pi, associate the parts as indicated by the schematic underneath.

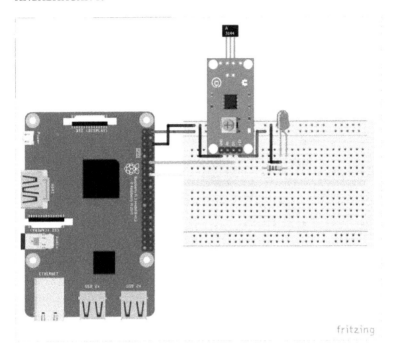

The Hall sensor utilized for this instructional exercise can give both simple and computerized values at the yield. Be that as it may, to streamline the instructional exercise, I chose to utilize the advanced worth since utilizing the simple yield will require the association of an ADC to the Raspberry Pi.

Python Code and Working Explanation:

The Python Code for this Hall Sensor venture is a straightforward one, we should simply to peruse the yield from the corridor sensor, and turn on or off the LED as needs be. The LED is to be turned on if the magnet is identified and it is to be killed something else.

Catalyst your Raspberry Pi and SSH into it utilizing putty (whenever associated in headless mode as am I). As normal with the majority of my tasks, I make a registry inside the home catalog where everything about each undertaking is put away so for this venture, we will make an index called lobby. If it's not too much problem note this is only an individual inclination to keep things composed.

Make the index utilizing;

mkdir hallsensor

Change index into the new registry just made and open a proofreader to make the python content utilizing;

cd hallsensor

pursued by;

nano hallsensorcode.py

When the supervisor opens, we type in the code for venture. I will do a concise breakdown of the code to show key ideas, and the total python code will be made accessible after that.

We start the code by bringing in the RPI.GPIO library which permits us compose python contents to interface with the raspberry pi GPIO pins.

```
import RPi.GPIO as gpio
```

Next we set the numbering design for the Rpi's GPIO that we will jump at the chance to utilize and impair GPIO alerts to permit free stream execution of the code.

```
gpio.setmode(gpio.BCM)

gpio.setwarnings(False)
```

We at that point set announce the GPIO pins to which the LED and the computerized yield of the corridor sensor is associated as per the BCM numbering chose.

```
hallpin = 2
```

```
ledpin = 3
```

Next, we set up the GPIO sticks as info or yield. The stick with which the LED is associated set as yield and the one to which the lobby sensor is associated set as info.

```
gpio.setup( hallpin, gpio.IN)

gpio.setup(ledpin, gpio.OUT)
```

With that done, we compose the principle part of the code, which is some time circle that continually assesses the yield from the lobby sensor and turns on the LED if a magnet is recognized and kills the LED when a magnet isn't distinguished.

```
while True:

    if(gpio.input(hallpin) == False):

        gpio.output(ledpin, True)

        print("magnet detected")

    else:
```

gpio.output(ledpin, False)

print("magnetic field not detected")

The total python code is given toward the finish of the undertaking.

```
pi@klempy: ~/hall

GNU nano 2.2.6            File: hallsensor.py

import RPi.GPIO as gpio


gpio.setmode(gpio.BCM)
gpio.setwarnings(False)

hallpin = 2
ledpin = 3

gpio.setup(hallpin, gpio.IN)
gpio.setup(ledpin, gpio.OUT)
gpio.output(ledpin, False)

while True:
        if(gpio.input(hallpin) == False):
                gpio.output(ledpin, True)
                print ("magnet detected!")
        else:
                gpio.output(ledpin, False)
```

Duplicate and Save the code and leave the editorial manager in the wake of composing it in utilizing;

CTRL + X pursued by y.

In the wake of sparing, go over your associations by and by and run the python content utilizing;

sudo python hallsensorcode.py

With the content running, at whatever point a magnet or anything attractive is carried near the corridor sensor, the LED lights up like appeared in the picture beneath.

From reed switches for a shrewd home to speedometers for a bike, there are a few overly cool stuffs that can be worked with this instructional exercise at the base. Don't hesitate to share any extend you intend to work in the remark segment underneath.

All check our past lobby sensor based tasks:

- DIY Speedometer utilizing Arduino and Processing Android App

- Computerized Speedometer and Odometer Circuit utilizing PIC Microcontroller

- Computer generated Reality utilizing Arduino as well as Processing
- Attractive Field Strength Measurement utilizing Arduino

Code

```
import RPi.GPIO as gpio
gpio.setmode(gpio.BCM)
gpio.setwarnings(False)
hallpin = 2
ledpin = 3
gpio.setup( hallpin, gpio.IN)
gpio.setup(ledpin, gpio.OUT)
gpio.output(ledpin, False)
while True:
  if(gpio.input(hallpin) == False):
    gpio.output(ledpin, True)
    print("magnet detected")
  else:
    gpio.output(ledpin, False)
    print("magnetic field not detected")
```

9. MPU6050 GYRO SENSOR INTERFACING WITH RASPBERRY PI

The MPU6050 sensor has numerous capacities over the single chip. It comprises a MEMS accelerometer, a MEMS gyro, as well as temperature sensor. This module is precise while changing over simple qualities to computerized on the grounds that it has a 16bit easy to advanced converter equipment for each channel. This module is competent to catch x, y and z channel simultaneously. It has an I2C interface to speak with the host controller. This MPU6050 module is a conservative chip having accelerometer as well as gyro. This is an exceptionally helpful gadget for some, applications like automatons, robots, movement sensors. It is likewise called Gyroscope or Triple hub accelerometer.

Here we are gonna to Interface this MPU6050 with Raspberry Pi and indicating the qualities over 16x2

LCD.

Required Components:

- Raspberry Pi
- 10K POT
- MPU-6050
- Breadboard
- Jumper wire
- Power supply

MPU6050 Gyro Sensor:

MPU-6050 is a 8 stick 6 hub gyro and accelerometer in a solitary chip. This module takes a shot at I2C sequential correspondence as a matter of course however it very well may be designed for SPI interface by arranging it register. For I2C this has SDA and SCL lines. Practically every one of the pins are multiworking however here we are continuing just with I2C mode pins.

Stick Configuration:

Vcc:- this stick is utilized for controlling the MPU6050 module as for ground

GND:- this is a ground stick

SDA:- SDA stick is utilized for information among controller and mpu6050 module

SCL:- SCL stick is utilized for clock input

XDA:- This is sensor I2C SDA Data line for designing and perusing from outer sensors ((discretionary) not utilized for our situation)

XCL:- This is sensor I2C SCL clock line for designing and perusing from outer sensors ((discretionary) not utilized for our situation)

ADO:- I2C Slave Address LSB (not pertinent for our situation)

INT:- Interrupt stick for sign of information prepared.

We have beforehand interfaced MPU6050 with Arduino.
Description:

Here, we are demonstrating temperature, gyro and accelerometer readings over LCD utilizing MPU6050 with Raspberry Pi. In case you are new to Raspberry Pi, at that point experience our Raspberry Pi instructional exercises segment and get the hang of beginning with Raspberry Pi.

In this venture, we have first demonstrated temperature esteem over LCD and after some time we show gyro esteems and afterward after some time we have accelerometer readings as appeared in the pictures underneath:

Circuit Diagram and Explanation:

The circuit graph, for interfacing MPU6050 with Raspberry Pi, is straightforward here we have utilized a LCD and MPU6050. A 10k pot is utilized for controlling the splendor of the LCD. Regarding MPU6050, we have completed 4 associations in which we have associated the 3.3v power supply as well as ground of MPU6050 to the 3.3v as well as ground of Raspberry Pi. SCL and SDA pins of MPU6050 is associated with Raspberry's physical stick 3(GPIO2) and stick 5 (GPIO3). LCD's RS, RW, and EN are legitimately associated with GPIO18, and 23 of raspberry pi. Information stick are legitimately associated with advanced stick number GPIO24, GPIO25, GPIO8, and GPIO7. Study interfacing LCD with Raspberry Pi here.

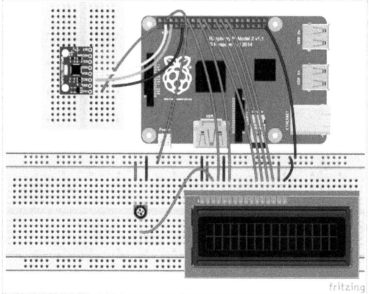

Configuring Raspberry Pi for MPU6050 Gyro sensor:

Before start programming, we have to empower i2c of Raspberry Pi by utilizing given technique:

Stage 1: Enable I2C correspondence

Before introducing Adafruit SSD1306 library we have to empower I2C correspondence in Raspberry Pi.

To do this sort in Raspberry Pi comfort:

sudo raspi-config

And afterward a blue screen will show up. Presently select interface choice

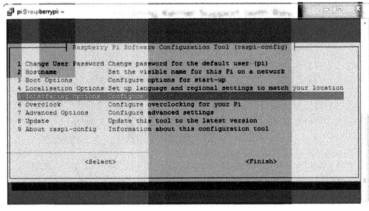

After this, we have to need to choose I2C

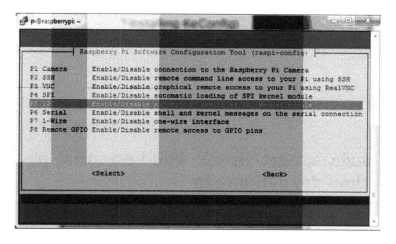

After this, we have to choose yes and press enter and afterward alright

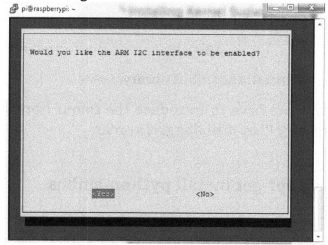

After this, we have to reboot raspberry pi by giving underneath order:

> **sodo reboot**

Stage 2: Install python-pip and GPIO Library

> **sudo apt-get install build-essential python-dev python-pip**

After this, we have to introduce raspberry pi GPIO library

> **sudo pip installs RPi.GPIO**

Stage 3: Install the smbus library

At last, we have to introduce the smbus library in Raspberry Pi by utilizing given order:

> **sudo apt-get install python-smbus**

```
pi@raspberrypi:~ $ sudo apt install python-smbus
Reading package lists... Done
Building dependency tree
Reading state information... Done
python-smbus is already the newest version.
0 upgraded, 0 newly installed, 0 to remove and 49 not upgraded.
pi@raspberrypi:~ $ pip install mpu6050-raspberrypi
```

Stage 4: Install the library MPU6050

After this we have to introduce MPU6050 library by utilizing given order

sudo pip install mpu6050

Presently we can discover model codes in the models. Client can test that code by legitimately transferring to the Raspberry Pi or modify it as per prerequisite. Here we have shown MPU6050's X, Y and Z pivot esteems on 16x2 LCD. You can locate the full Python Code toward the finish of the Tutorial.
Programming Explanation:

Complete Python Code is given toward the end here we are clarifying scarcely any significant piece of the code.

In Python Program, we have imported some necessary library like time, smbus, as well as GPIO.

import smbus

```
import time

import RPi.GPIO as gpio
```

After this, we have to take some enlist address to arrange MPU6050 and for getting values from the equivalent. We have additionally taken a few factors for adjusting and introducing transport for I2C.

```
PWR_M  = 0x6B

DIV  = 0x19

CONFIG    = 0x1A

GYRO_CONFIG = 0x1B

INT_EN  = 0x38

ACCEL_X = 0x3B

ACCEL_Y = 0x3D

ACCEL_Z = 0x3F

GYRO_X  = 0x43

GYRO_Y  = 0x45
```

```
GYRO_Z = 0x47

TEMP = 0x41

bus = smbus.SMBus(1)

Device_Address = 0x68  # device address

AxCal=0

AyCal=0

AzCal=0

GxCal=0

GyCal=0

GzCal=0
```

At that point we have kept in touch with certain capacities for Driving 16x2LCD like def start(), def cmd(ch), def write(ch), def Print(str), def clear() and so forth. You can additionally check Interfacing of LCD with Raspberry Pi.

After this, we have to introduce the MPU6050 Module

```python
def InitMPU():

    bus.write_byte_data(Device_Address,
DIV, 7)

    bus.write_byte_data(Device_Address,
PWR_M, 1)

    bus.write_byte_data(Device_Address,
CONFIG, 0)

    bus.write_byte_data(Device_Address,
GYRO_CONFIG, 24)

    bus.write_byte_data(Device_Address,
INT_EN, 1)

    time.sleep(1)
```

After this, we have to keep in touch with certain capacities to peruse esteems from MPU6050 and show them to LCD. Given capacity is utilized to peruse information from MPU6050

```python
def readMPU(addr):
```

```
high = bus.read_byte_data(Device_Ad-
dress, addr)

low = bus.read_byte_data(Device_Ad-
dress, addr+1)

value = ((high << 8) | low)

if(value > 32768):

    value = value - 65536

return value
```

Given capacity is utilized to understand accelerometer and gyro meter information

```
def accel():

    x = readMPU(ACCEL_X)

    y = readMPU(ACCEL_Y)

    z = readMPU(ACCEL_Z)

    Ax = (x/16384.0-AxCal)
```

```python
    Ay = (y/16384.0-AyCal)

    Az = (z/16384.0-AzCal)

    #print "X="+str(Ax)

    display(Ax,Ay,Az)

    time.sleep(.01)
def gyro():

    global GxCal

    global GyCal

    global GzCal

    x = readMPU(GYRO_X)

    y = readMPU(GYRO_Y)

    z = readMPU(GYRO_Z)

    Gx = x/131.0 - GxCal

    Gy = y/131.0 - GyCal
```

```
Gz = z/131.0 - GzCal

#print "X="+str(Gx)

display(Gx,Gy,Gz)

time.sleep(.01)
```

After this, we have composed a temperature under-standing capacity

```
def temp():

    tempRow=readMPU(TEMP)

    tempC=(tempRow / 340.0) + 36.53

    tempC="%.2f" %tempC

    print tempC

    setCursor(0,0)

    Print("Temp: ")

    Print(str(tempC))
```

```
time.sleep(.2)
```

def align() work is utilized to adjust the MPU6050 and def show() work is utilized to show the qualities on LCD. Check these capacities in the full code given underneath.

After this, we have started the LCD, introduce and adjust the MPU6050 and afterward in while circle we have called all the each of the three arrangement of qualities from MPU-temperature, accelerometer and gyro and demonstrated them over LCD.

```
begin();

Print("MPU6050 Interface")

setCursor(0,1)

Print("Hello world")

time.sleep(2)

InitMPU()

calibrate()

while 1:
```

```
InitMPU()

clear()

for i in range(20):

  temp()

clear()

Print("Accel")

time.sleep(1)

for i in range(30):

  accel()

clear()

Print("Gyro")

time.sleep(1)

for i in range(30):

gyro()
```

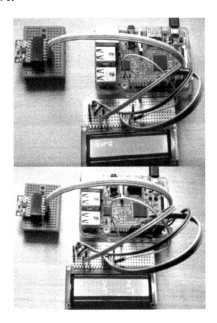

MPU6050 gyro and accelerometer both are utilized to distinguish the position and direction of any gadget. Gyro utilizes earth gravity to decide the x,y and z-hub positions and accelerometer distinguishes dependent on the pace of the difference in development. We previously utilized the accelerometer with Arduino in a significant number of our undertakings like:

- Accelerometer Based Hand Gesture Controlled Robot

- Arduino Based Vehicle Accident Alert System

- Quake Detector Alarm utilizing Arduino

Code

```
import smbus
import time
import RPi.GPIO as gpio
PWR_M  = 0x6B
DIV  = 0x19
CONFIG     = 0x1A
GYRO_CONFIG = 0x1B
INT_EN   = 0x38
ACCEL_X = 0x3B
ACCEL_Y = 0x3D
ACCEL_Z = 0x3F
GYRO_X  = 0x43
GYRO_Y  = 0x45
GYRO_Z  = 0x47
TEMP = 0x41
bus = smbus.SMBus(1)
Device_Address = 0x68   # device address
AxCal=0
AyCal=0
AzCal=0
GxCal=0
GyCal=0
GzCal=0
RS =18
```

```
EN =23
D4 =24
D5 =25
D6 =8
D7 =7
gpio.setwarnings(False)
gpio.setmode(gpio.BCM)
gpio.setup(RS, gpio.OUT)
gpio.setup(EN, gpio.OUT)
gpio.setup(D4, gpio.OUT)
gpio.setup(D5, gpio.OUT)
gpio.setup(D6, gpio.OUT)
gpio.setup(D7, gpio.OUT)
def begin():
  cmd(0x33)
  cmd(0x32)
  cmd(0x06)
  cmd(0x0C)
  cmd(0x28)
  cmd(0x01)
  time.sleep(0.0005)
def cmd(ch):
  gpio.output(RS, 0)
  gpio.output(D4, 0)
  gpio.output(D5, 0)
  gpio.output(D6, 0)
  gpio.output(D7, 0)
```

```python
if ch&0x10==0x10:
 gpio.output(D4, 1)
if ch&0x20==0x20:
 gpio.output(D5, 1)
if ch&0x40==0x40:
 gpio.output(D6, 1)
if ch&0x80==0x80:
 gpio.output(D7, 1)
gpio.output(EN, 1)
time.sleep(0.005)
gpio.output(EN, 0)
# Low bits
gpio.output(D4, 0)
gpio.output(D5, 0)
gpio.output(D6, 0)
gpio.output(D7, 0)
if ch&0x01==0x01:
 gpio.output(D4, 1)
if ch&0x02==0x02:
 gpio.output(D5, 1)
if ch&0x04==0x04:
 gpio.output(D6, 1)
if ch&0x08==0x08:
 gpio.output(D7, 1)
gpio.output(EN, 1)
time.sleep(0.005)
gpio.output(EN, 0)
```

```
def write(ch):
 gpio.output(RS, 1)
 gpio.output(D4, 0)
 gpio.output(D5, 0)
 gpio.output(D6, 0)
 gpio.output(D7, 0)
 if ch&0x10==0x10:
  gpio.output(D4, 1)
 if ch&0x20==0x20:
  gpio.output(D5, 1)
 if ch&0x40==0x40:
  gpio.output(D6, 1)
 if ch&0x80==0x80:
  gpio.output(D7, 1)
 gpio.output(EN, 1)
 time.sleep(0.005)
 gpio.output(EN, 0)
 # Low bits
 gpio.output(D4, 0)
 gpio.output(D5, 0)
 gpio.output(D6, 0)
 gpio.output(D7, 0)
 if ch&0x01==0x01:
  gpio.output(D4, 1)
 if ch&0x02==0x02:
  gpio.output(D5, 1)
 if ch&0x04==0x04:
```

```
 gpio.output(D6, 1)
 if ch&0x08==0x08:
  gpio.output(D7, 1)
 gpio.output(EN, 1)
 time.sleep(0.005)
 gpio.output(EN, 0)
def clear():
 cmd(0x01)
def Print(Str):
 l=0;
 l=len(Str)
 for i in range(l):
  write(ord(Str[i]))
def setCursor(x,y):
    if y == 0:
        n=128+x
    elif y == 1:
        n=192+x
    cmd(n)
def InitMPU():
bus.write_byte_data(Device_Address, DIV, 7)
bus.write_byte_data(Device_Address,
PWR_M, 1)
bus.write_byte_data(Device_Address,   CON-
FIG, 0)
bus.write_byte_data(Device_Address,
GYRO_CONFIG, 24)
```

```
bus.write_byte_data(Device_Address,
INT_EN, 1)
time.sleep(1)
def display(x,y,z):
   x=x*100
   y=y*100
   z=z*100
   x= "%d" %x
   y= "%d" %y
   z= "%d" %z
   setCursor(0,0)
   Print("X    Y    Z")
   setCursor(0,1)
   Print(str(x))
   Print(" ")
   setCursor(6,1)
   Print(str(y))
   Print(" ")
   setCursor(12,1)
   Print(str(z))
   Print(" ")
   print x
   print y
   print z
def readMPU(addr):
high = bus.read_byte_data(Device_Address,
addr)
```

```
low  =  bus.read_byte_data(Device_Address,
addr+1)
value = ((high << 8) | low)
if(value > 32768):
value = value - 65536
return value
def accel():
x = readMPU(ACCEL_X)
y = readMPU(ACCEL_Y)
z = readMPU(ACCEL_Z)
Ax = (x/16384.0-AxCal)
Ay = (y/16384.0-AyCal)
Az = (z/16384.0-AzCal)
#print "X="+str(Ax)
display(Ax,Ay,Az)
time.sleep(.01)
def gyro():
   global GxCal
   global GyCal
   global GzCal
   x = readMPU(GYRO_X)
   y = readMPU(GYRO_Y)
   z = readMPU(GYRO_Z)
   Gx = x/131.0 - GxCal
   Gy = y/131.0 - GyCal
   Gz = z/131.0 - GzCal
   #print "X="+str(Gx)
```

```
    display(Gx,Gy,Gz)
    time.sleep(.01)
def temp():
 tempRow=readMPU(TEMP)
 tempC=(tempRow / 340.0) + 36.53
 tempC="%.2f" %tempC
 print tempC
 setCursor(0,0)
 Print("Temp: ")
 Print(str(tempC))
 time.sleep(.2)
def calibrate():
 clear()
 Print("Calibrate....")
 global AxCal
 global AyCal
 global AzCal
 x=0
 y=0
 z=0
 for i in range(50):
    x = x + readMPU(ACCEL_X)
    y = y + readMPU(ACCEL_Y)
    z = z + readMPU(ACCEL_Z)
 x= x/50
 y= y/50
 z= z/50
```

```
AxCal = x/16384.0
AyCal = y/16384.0
AzCal = z/16384.0
print AxCal
print AyCal
print AzCal
global GxCal
global GyCal
global GzCal
x=0
y=0
z=0
for i in range(50):
  x = x + readMPU(GYRO_X)
  y = y + readMPU(GYRO_Y)
  z = z + readMPU(GYRO_Z)
x= x/50
y= y/50
z= z/50
GxCal = x/131.0
GyCal = y/131.0
GzCal = z/131.0
print GxCal
print GyCal
print GzCal
begin();
Print("MPU6050 Interface")
```

```
setCursor(0,1)
Print("Hello world")
time.sleep(2)
InitMPU()
calibrate()
while 1:
 InitMPU()
 clear()
 for i in range(20):
  temp()
 clear()
 Print("Accel")
 time.sleep(1)
 for i in range(30):
  accel()
 clear()
 Print("Gyro")
 time.sleep(1)
 for i in range(30):
  gyro()
```

❖ ❖ ❖

10. INTERFACING SSD1306 OLED DISPLAY WITH RASPBERRY PI

A large portion of us would be comfortable with the 16×2 Dot network LCD show that is utilized in the vast majority of the ventures to show some data to the client. Be that as it may, these LCD shows have a great deal of impediments. In this instructional exercise, we will find out about OLED show and how to utilize them with Raspberry Pi. There are loads of kinds of OLED shows accessible in the market and there are bunches of approaches to make them work. We have just utilized 7 Pin OLED with Arduino.

Hardware Required:

- 128×64 Organic Light Emitting Diode display Module (SSD1306)
- Breadboard
- Raspberry Pi

- Power supply
- Connecting Wires

Getting to know about OLED Displays:

The term OLED means "Natural Light transmitting diode" it utilizes a similar innovation that is utilized in the vast majority of our TVs however has less pixels contrasted with them. It is genuine enjoyable to have these cool looking presentation modules to be interfaced with the Raspberry Pi since it will make our undertakings look cool. We have secured a full Article on OLED showcases and its sorts here. Here, we are utilizing a Monochrome 4-stick SSD1306 0.96" OLED show. This LCD can just work with the I2C mode.

The following are the associations of OLED with Raspberry pi:?

OLED Pin	RPI Pin
VCC	3.3v
GND	GND
SDA	SDA (Physical pin 3)
SCL	SCL (Physical pin 5)

Circuit Diagram:

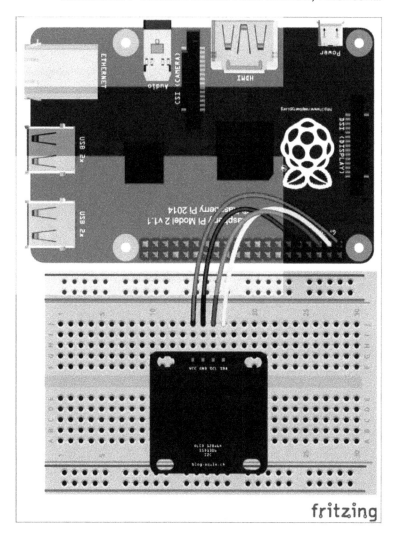

Connecting OLED with Raspberry Pi:

RPI people group has just given us a great deal of Libraries which can be straightforwardly used to make this much less complex. I evaluated a couple of libraries and found that the Adafruit_SSD1306 OLED Library was anything but difficult to utilize and has a bunch of graphical choices thus we will utilize the equivalent in this instructional exercise.

Stage 1: Enable I2C correspondence

Before introducing Adafruit SSD1306 library we have to empower I2C correspondence in Raspberry Pi.

To do this sort in Raspberry Pi comfort:

sudo raspi-config

And afterward a blue screen will show up. Presently select interface choice

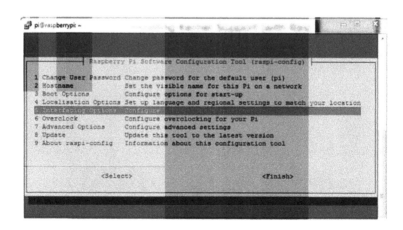

After this, we have to need to choose I2C

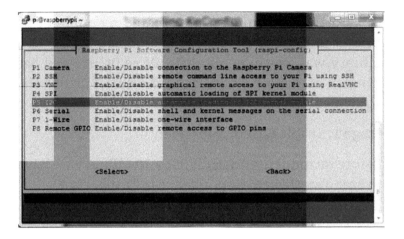

After this, we have to choose yes and press enter and afterward alright

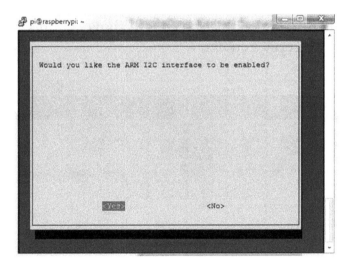

After this, we have to reboot raspberry pi by giving beneath direction:

sodo reboot

Stage 2: Find OLED I2C address and update it

At that point we have to discover OLED I2C address by utilizing given direction and you will see a hex location.

sudo i2cdetect –y 1

At that point update Raspberry Pi utilizing given order:

sudo apt-get update

Stage 3: Install python-pip and GPIO Library

After this we have to introduce pip by utilizing given order:

```
sudo apt-get install build-essential py-
thon-dev python-pip
```

What's more, introduce Raspberry Pi GPIO library

```
sudo pip installs RPi.GPIO
```

Stage 4: Install the Python Imaging Library and smbus library

At last, we have to introduce the Python Imaging Library and smbus library in Raspberry Pi by utilizing given order:

```
sudo apt-get install python-imaging py-
thon-smbus
```

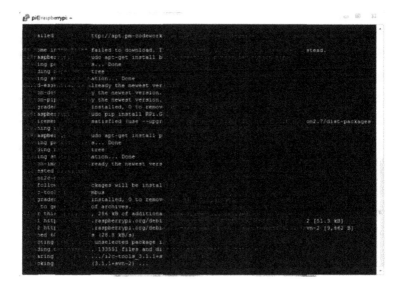

Stage 5: introduce the Adafruit SSD1306 python library

Presently its opportunity to introduce the Adafruit SSD1306 python library code and models by utilizing given directions:

sudo apt-get install git

git clone https://github.com/adafruit/ Adafruit_Python_SSD1306.git

cd Adafruit_Python_SSD1306

sudo python setup.py install

Presently client can discover the code of OLED interfacing in Raspberry Pi and you can play straightforwardly or tweak it yourself. Here we have modified a model code for exhibit. You can discover full Python code toward the finish of the article.

Programming Explanation:

Programming part for interfacing OLED with RPi venture is simple. to begin with, we have to import some fundamental libraries.

import time

import Adafruit_GPIO.SPI as SPI

import Adafruit_SSD1306

from PIL import Image

from PIL import ImageDraw

```python
from PIL import ImageFont

import subprocess
```

After this instate the showcase

```python
RST = 0

disp = Adafruit_SSD1306.SSD1306_128_64(rst=RST)

disp.begin()

disp.clear()

disp.display()

width = disp.width

height = disp.height

image1 = Image.new('1', (width, height))

draw = ImageDraw.Draw(image1)

draw.rectangle((0,0,width,height), outline=0, fill=0)
```

```
padding = -2

top = padding

bottom = height-padding

x = 0

font = ImageFont.load_default()
```

After this, we can send information or picture to OLED by utilizing given code

```
# Write two lines of text.

disp.clear()

disp.display()

draw.text((x, top),     "OLED Interfacing " ,
font=font, fill=255)

draw.text((x,  top+8),        "Hello  world",
font=font, fill=255)

draw.text((x, top+16),   "For more Videos",
font=font, fill=255)
```

```python
draw.text((x,   top+25),        "Visit   at",
font=font, fill=255)

draw.text((x,                         top
+34),        "www.helloo_its_me_anbazha-
gan.com",  font=font, fill=255)

# Display image.

disp.image(image1)

disp.display()

time.sleep(2)

if disp.height == 64:

  image   =   Image.open('img1.png').con-
vert('1')

else:

  image   =   Image.open('img1.png').con-
vert('1')

disp.image(image)

disp.display()
```

```
time.sleep(2)

if disp.height == 64:

    image    =    Image.open('img3.jpg').con-
vert('1')

else:

    image    =    Image.open('img3.jpg').con-
vert('1')
```

This OLED comes in two variations one is 128*32 and other is 128*64 so the client can choose anybody as needs be while instating OLED. Here we have composed this code for both. The client needs to just instate OLED for 128*64 pixel like:

```
disp        =        Adafruit_SSD1306.SS-
D1306_128_64(rst=RST)
```

All the code and capacities are straightforward and no further clarification is required. Simply begin and have a go at playing with stature, width and pictures and attempt some different capacities to make some increasingly cool geometric figures.

Full python code is given beneath and here you discover the pictures which we have utilized in this program.

Likewise check OLED Interfacing with Arduino.

Code

```
import time
import Adafruit_GPIO.SPI as SPI
import Adafruit_SSD1306
from PIL import Image
from PIL import ImageDraw
from PIL import ImageFont
import subprocess
RST = 0
disp             =             Adafruit_SSD1306.SS-
D1306_128_64(rst=RST)
disp.begin()
disp.clear()
disp.display()
width = disp.width
height = disp.height
image1 = Image.new('1', (width, height))
draw = ImageDraw.Draw(image1)
draw.rectangle((0,0,width,height),        out-
line=0, fill=0)
padding = -2
```

```
top = padding
bottom = height-padding
x = 0
font = ImageFont.load_default()
while True:
    draw.rectangle((0,0,width,height), out-
line=0, fill=0)
  # Write two lines of text.
  disp.clear()
  disp.display()
  draw.text((x, top),      "OLED Interfacing " ,
font=font, fill=255)
    draw.text((x, top+8),      "Hello world",
font=font, fill=255)
  draw.text((x, top+16),   "For more Videos",
font=font, fill=255)
      draw.text((x, top+25),       "Visit at",
font=font, fill=255)
  draw.text((x, top+34),   "www.Its_me_an-
bazhagan.com", font=font, fill=255)
  # Display image.
  disp.image(image1)
  disp.display()
  time.sleep(2)
  if disp.height == 64:
      image = Image.open('img1.png').con-
```

```
vert('1')
  else:
      image = Image.open('img1.png').con-
vert('1')
  disp.image(image)
  disp.display()
  time.sleep(2)
  if disp.height == 64:
      image = Image.open('img3.jpg').con-
vert('1')
  else:
      image = Image.open('img3.jpg').con-
vert('1')
  disp.image(image)
  disp.display()
  time.sleep(2)
  if disp.height == 64:
      image = Image.open('img4.jpg').con-
vert('1')
  else:
      image = Image.open('img4.jpg').con-
vert('1')
  disp.image(image)
  disp.display()
  time.sleep(2)
```

Thank You !!!